G000257727

"James Poch is the real deal. He is pas
his own life, in his family, and in l
everyday wisdom and real-life stories
ciple-making looks like in practice –
Read it and pass it on."

— **Ric Thorpe, Bishop of Islington, London**
Priest in Charge, St Edmund & St Mary Woolnoth.

"There are no short cuts to our Jesus-given mandate to go and make
disciples. It is an urgent, and often difficult, task. Written with vulnerability and earthed with gritty testimonies, the following pages are not
discipleship theory. Rather the author presents the reality of what discipleship practically looks like day to day. You will be inspired and
further equipped for this essential task as you read."

— **Martin Durham**
*Director of K180, European Director for the International Leadership
Institute, and chair of the leadership team of the Billy Graham Evangelis-
tic Association 'Emerging Evangelists Institute'.*

"True discipleship seems to have faded over the years, along with spiritual
grit. As we look at James and Ruth Poch we see a couple who have picked
up their cross and chosen to unwaveringly follow Jesus along the narrow,
at times rocky road, through gates of betrayal and dark valley times.
Giving up was not an option. They chose to say 'YES' to Jesus and 'NO'
to compromise. They chose to swim upstream, no matter the cost. Today
we watch them discipling and parenting many young people into the
fullness of what God has for each one of them. They live out their lives
daily demonstrating spiritual grit. This book is a must-read for every
leader and every believer in the body of Christ as it encourages, provokes
and reminds us how vital true discipleship is in the life of the local church
and in each of our lives. Together we are so much stronger."

Jesus said: "Go therefore and make disciples of all the nations,
baptizing them in the name of the Father and of the Son and of the
Holy Spirit."

— **Tich and Joan Smith**
Co-Founders of LIV children's village, South Africa.

I love the idea of 'Holy Grit!' Having known James for many years, he definitely knows what he is talking about here! His book is a radical call to go beyond the superficial and the simple, to press in, "to know Him and the power of His resurrection." I was challenged, motivated and inspired... It is a much needed book.

— **JENNIFER REES LARCOMBE**
Author and founder of the Beauty From Ashes Trust.

People often talk about discipleship but James has gone further. Not only has he lived out his life as a disciple but he has delved deep into what discipleship looks like in the 21st Century, having helped others become followers of Jesus. Holy Grit unpacks discipleship with a biblical bedrock and a wealth of wisdom, experience and passion. James is raw and honest and his writing is enriched with real life stories from young people he has worked with at regen Church. I invite you to read this book, to be challenged in your own walk with God and better equipped to join Jesus in making disciples.

— **ANDY FROST**
Director of Share Jesus International and Head of the London Mission Collective.

This book is a must-read for anyone interested in discipleship. Filled with true life stories of ordinary people who have transitioned into making the extraordinary commitment of following Jesus above everything else, it has brilliant wisdom on how mentoring can be used by God to transform lives. James Poch has lived this out for years, and you can now learn from that experience on what topics you should focus on to mentor new believers into mature Christians.

— **MARK WILLIAMSON**
Co-founder and co-director of One Rock. He leads the curriculum development on Discerning Vision and Leadership Skills and is an Author and Associate Minister with Fresh Expressions. He also leads the Prayer for London movement.

HOLY GRIT

Gaining Traction on Life's Journey with Jesus

James Poch

Published by Zaccmedia
www.zaccmedia.com

Published December 2017

ISBN: 978-1-911211-73-0

Cover design by Ben Spearman.

ACKNOWLEDGEMENTS

To all my friends and co-workers in the gospel – the regeneration leadership team – Ruth Poch, Alicia Edmund, Ben Poch, Ben Spearman, Jason Piper, Naomi Fowler, Sam Fowler, and Richard Shaw. This book would have never been in print without your loving support and guidance over these past three years. Thanks so much for all your input into this book and for believing I could do it. Love you guys!

Thank you to Ben Spearman and Rebecca Poch for their helpful edits and Ben for your tireless work on the great cover design.

I would also like to thank Rev Rod Green for his early suggestions and Bishop Ric Thorpe for his later suggestions. You have both been an encouraging voice in this project.

Finally and gratefully, I am indebted to my amazing wife, Ruth Poch who has read my manuscript several times over. I greatly value your wisdom and insight in the long and sometimes painful journey of writing this book. I am so blessed to have you as my co-worker in the gospel.

For my great-grandmother, Anna Cavitch and my grandmothers, Eileen Evans and Jessica Poch. Although they have passed on, I have never doubted their prayers for me have and are being answered.

CONTENTS

THE JOURNEY IS THE REWARD

Chinese proverb

INTRODUCTION

THE PURPOSE OF THIS BOOK is twofold. It is written to encourage you to be a better disciple, and a better discipler of others. I haven't separated out these two important elements of the Christian faith in the chapters too much because they are so intricately interwoven. Every Christian is, or should be, a disciple, and every Christian should be discipling someone else. Disciples and disciplers share the journey of becoming more like Jesus Christ every day.

There can be no substitute for discipleship in the Church. Over seventy years ago, Dietrich Bonhoeffer wrote:

> Christianity without the living Christ is inevitably Christianity without discipleship, and Christianity without discipleship is always Christianity without Christ.
>
> Dietrich Bonhoeffer[1]

In many ways, our leadership team at regeneration Church has had to learn the hard way how essential Christianity with the living Christ is for our worshipping community.

At the inception of regeneration, there was a real buzz about what the church could do and be. We planted it in 2004 with just a handful of young people, four of them being our own sons. We were doing something new and largely unexplored, as far as local Methodism was concerned. There was a sense of excitement and challenge about what God was doing. Any young person who possessed any talent for music would be welcomed to be a part of our fledgling band. Our young leaders were, on average, seventeen years old. We didn't really have much criteria for church leadership or the band, apart from the basic skills necessary and a willingness to serve. Great things were happening, services were growing and young people were becoming Christians and attending church regularly. Good reports about what we were doing with young people travelled far and wide, but there was just one problem – spiritually, we were a mile wide and an inch deep.

At first glance everything looked terrific, but below the surface things were not as healthy as they appeared – cracks started to appear. After a series of revelations, it became clear that we could not carry on assimilating anyone with talent into our band. There were moral failures among some of the members which led to some of them stepping down. In one week the band went from being OK to plain awful. I announced from the platform that we wouldn't be carrying on as usual and that some of the changes meant that we would be worshipping differently. I expounded the importance of focusing on the worship and not the performance of the now decimated band. Someone in the congregation commented later that upon hearing my short speech she thought, "This worship band is going to be bad," and after hearing us play, pronounced, "and it was."

We were stripped of our talented musicians and the band sounded terrible, but at least we sounded terrible for the right reason. We were sacrificing giftedness on stage for integrity across the board, and although it was a painful thing to do, we were able to realise the rewards of holding to a moral standard later.

More cracks started to appear – not a single crack, but many. Another 'crack' that appeared so painfully and swiftly was the arrest of our two eldest sons who were caught tagging a shopfront with a felt-tip marker. A minor misdemeanour, one might think, but the revelations that followed on from that event were staggering. We consequently discovered that our sons were heavily into illegal graffiti and other aspects of gang culture. What ultimately came out of that seemingly hopeless situation has directed our church into a lives-transforming journey of intentional discipleship that has deepened our dependency on God and one another.

As a result of our new-found emphasis on discipleship, we have seen great spiritual growth in the character and leadership of our young people. Equally, we have realised the benefits in people of all ages who have taken up Jesus' call to "Come and follow me". The very nature of this new-found emphasis on discipleship has had a long-lasting effect on our family as well. It took a few years for our two eldest sons to break free from their addiction to graffiti, but now they are serving God faithfully in tremendous ways.

One prayer meeting after all of these difficult events, we had a time of waiting on God to listen for what he might wish to say to us. After a few minutes of silence, one young man offered that he had only one word he felt might be from God: "Discipleship." Ruth, and I were encouraged by this, as we had only just been talking about the need for a more disciplined and focused emphasis on discipleship just a short while before. That single word started us on a journey to explore what this meant for our ragtag band of young Jesus followers. Of course, we knew what discipleship looked like in the New Testament when Jesus called his twelve, mainly young disciples together to create a movement which would turn the world upside down. What we didn't know then was what discipleship would look like in the twenty-first century among a growing group of young people who really didn't have much experience of church. We set out on a thrilling and equally arduous journey of discovery into the depths of what discipleship meant in our context. This is our story and all we have learned about disciple-ship along the way.

No matter how old we get, we will always be learning more about becoming like Jesus. The best learning we will ever gain will come through our daily walk with him. Nothing can compare with journeying through life with Christ. This book is about just that – journeying with Jesus and learning how to do life his way, no matter how difficult that may prove to be. I pray you will be challenged by what you read, and my hope is that you will be inspired to get stuck in even more with the loving, learning and doing that being a Christ-follower demands. Trust God in the journey. No matter how hard the climbs in your life get, or how harrowing the steep descents are, he will never abandon you. He has written your name on the palms of his hands. You are his and he holds you fast.

3 YEARS, 11 MONTHS
AND 15 DAYS

It ought to be the business of every day to prepare for our last day.

> Matthew Henry (1662–1714)

There are two days on my calendar – "Today" and "That Day".

> Martin Luther (1483–1546)

When it comes to physical, spiritual, emotional, or relational health, it will always cost you more if you don't start now.

> Brad Bridges[2]

O N 5 AUGUST 1967, MY MOM recorded the following story about me in my baby book:

> While questioning Daddy about Jesus' death on the cross, Jamie was overwhelmed to hear that Jesus loved him so much that with tears in his eyes he said, "Thank you," looking at his father.

I asked him if he would like Jesus to come into his heart and he said, "Yes, and will he come into the room right now and come into my heart?" I prayed and he repeated after me, when he finished he laughed till he was at the verge of tears and when I asked him how he felt he said, "Jesus is in my heart right now!"

Praise the Lord, as I believe his child-like faith has made him a true child of God and how wonderful at such a tender age of 3 years, 11 months and 15 days he found what has been hid from the wise and the prudent. May God use his life for the glory of Jesus and if it be his will, call him into the ministry.

They say big doors swing on small hinges. Well, that small prayer by a little boy, not quite four years old, has opened big doors of opportunity for me over the last fifty-three years of my life. I've never regretted the decision made then and I'm not sure I even remember making it. But that squeaky little prayer started me on a journey with Christ that has given me wonderful opportunities to tell people in many different parts of the world about the good news of Jesus Christ. I've had the pleasure and honour of sharing my faith with so many people and have had the blessing of starting regeneration Church from scratch with Ruth.

I could go on telling my story here, but this is not the book for that. Suffice to say, my life has been a long journey of faith. I have never walked alone. Jesus has been with me every step of the way – through the highs and lows of life, the birthday parties, school years, jobs, relationships, and seasons of illness. He's been with me through my marriage to Ruth, my trying to be a great father, and failing so many times to reach that goal. When I despaired of life in my teens and wondered if God cared, he was there. When I said "No" to him in my times of disobedience, he was there, waiting patiently for me to get with the plan. When I realised the error of my ways and said "Yes" to him, he was there too. I trusted him. I had to keep going back to him. There was nothing else; there was no one else who could lead me to wholeness, only the one who called himself "The Way, the Truth, and the Life". He who is "the Way" calls us to a life of never-ending daily discipleship, and that is what this book is all about.

ONE

LEARNERS AND DOERS

Oh, that we might know the Lord!
Let us press on to know him.
He will respond to us as surely as the arrival of dawn
or the coming of rains in early spring.

Hosea 6:3 (NLT)

The New Testament is a book about disciples, by
disciples, and for disciples of Jesus.

Dallas Willard[3]

TWO YOUNG MEN WHO CAME to our church for a while
were talking to one of our leaders about the high
value we place on discipleship at regen. One erroneously
offered, "It's not about us having to change, Jesus didn't
ask us to do that, he did it all on the cross." The other said
he didn't think discipleship was for him. It is tragic that
these two guys viewed discipleship in such a warped way.

1

Discipleship is for *every* Christian – no exceptions. Suffice to say, those young men drifted away from the church and are not presently living for Jesus.

It only takes a quick glance at any of the four Gospels to see that discipleship was very much Jesus' 'thing'. It was high on his agenda. In fact, it was like the Mount Everest of his agenda. He shared the whole of his ministry with twelve guys. The other New Testament books have an understanding, assumed or otherwise, that those who call themselves Christians will be disciples of Jesus.

You may even be surprised to know that the word 'Christian' only appears three times in the Bible but the word 'disciple' occurs not three times, but over 260 times throughout the New Testament. This gives good reason to place a high value upon it.

Becoming a disciple is not about signing up to a programme, adhering to a long list of dos and don'ts, or about simply doing good deeds. Being a disciple of Jesus is about growing to be like him, living a Spirit-filled lifestyle; one that is often at cross purposes with modern-day values.

Before we go any further, let's unpack what the word 'disciple' means. The word in the Greek, in which the New Testament was written, is *mathetes* which literally means 'learner'. If you attend a church and are learning, you are on your way to being a disciple – but that is only part of what being a disciple is about. Throughout the New Testament, there is an expectation that Christians will have head knowledge of what is right and wrong. Even more than that, there is an expectancy that we will actively do what the Bible commands by the power of the Holy Spirit. A disciple is far more than a learner; they are followers too, devoted to the teachings of Jesus, making them their rule of life.

> Don't just listen to the word. You fool your-selves if you do that. You must do what it says. Suppose someone listens to the word but doesn't do what it says. Then they are like a person who looks at their face in a mirror. After looking at themselves, they leave. And right away they forget what they look like. But suppose someone takes a good look at the perfect law that gives freedom. And they keep looking at it. Suppose they don't forget what they've heard, but they do what the law says. Then this person will be blessed in what they do.
>
> James 1:22–25 (NIRV)

Learning and doing go hand in hand in God's Kingdom. God has no interest in us simply letting us fill our heads with reams of knowledge about how to live. We have to channel the truth of what we are learning into loving, purposeful action so that we will become, as C.S. Lewis puts it, 'a little Christ'.

> Now the whole offer which Christianity makes is this: that we can, if we let God have His way, come to share in the life of Christ … He came to this world and became a man in order to spread to other men the

kind of life He has – by what I call "good infection." Every Christian is to become a little Christ. The whole purpose of becoming a Christian is simply nothing else.

C.S. Lewis[4]

If we are the 'little Christs' Lewis is talking about, we will have the same characteristics as Jesus. Our actions will identify us by the way we are living. Jesus nailed it when he delivered his Sermon on the Mount to his disciples and the crowds who followed him:

> Beware of false prophets who come disguised as harmless sheep but are really vicious wolves. You can identify them by their fruit, that is, by the way they act. Can you pick grapes from thornbushes, or figs from thistles? A good tree produces good fruit, and a bad tree produces bad fruit. A good tree can't produce bad fruit, and a bad tree can't produce good fruit. So every tree that does not produce good fruit is chopped down and thrown into the fire. Yes, just as you can identify a tree by its fruit, so you can identify people by their actions.
>
> Matthew 7:15–20 (NLT)

These are strong words. Jesus doesn't pull any punches when he talks about how we should be living as Christians. This is because a crucial part of the Kingdom of God is about right living. If we fail to get this right, we are simply a bunch of religious people pretending to be righteous but doing little that *is* right. Jesus remarked that these kinds of people are "like clouds blowing over the land without giving any rain" (Jude 12, NLT). We live in a world with people who are thirsty for authenticity, so why would we not offer them the Water of Life they desperately need? If we are not actively engaging ourselves with the Word of God by doing what it says, then we are like clouds that don't rain. We hold out the promise of something refreshing, but when it comes time to deliver the goods we are empty, leaving us incapable of quenching the thirst of people who need the Water of Life. Jesus said, "If anyone believes in me, rivers of living water will flow out from that person's heart, as the Scripture says" (John 7:38).

Many people believe in Jesus, but not everyone has "rivers of living water" flowing out of them. I was one of those people. I believed in Jesus, I prayed and read my Bible occasionally, but my life wasn't reflecting a passion for the Son of God's mission in the world. I was a nice, lukewarm Christian. This was not what God had in mind when he created me. God expects a decent return on what he's invested in me. He invested the life of his Son for my life. Is it any wonder he is expecting a high return from me in the way I live and share my faith with others?

In that lukewarm season of my life, I opened the channel of my heart just enough to permit a trickle of God's living water to dribble into me, but that certainly wasn't allowing for a river of living water to pour out of me to a desperate world. Deep inside I knew there was something more, something to fill that gnawing empty feeling, but I couldn't seem to find it. It took me some time to find out what it was that I needed to fill me up to overflowing. I am going to share with you what I've learned to get that flow going from a trickle to something more like God intended. It hasn't been easy, but it certainly has been an adventure.

God intends for his Spirit to pour into our lives, cleansing and changing us from the inside out. We in turn become a channel for the same flow in order that others too would receive the Water of Life that is Jesus Christ.

What is it going to take to get the wild river flowing? That is what we are going to explore in the next chapter.

T W O

TRUE GRIT

The best measure of a spiritual life is not its ecstasies but its obedience.

Oswald Chambers

Then Jesus said to his followers, "If people want to follow me, they must give up the things they want. They must be willing even to give up their lives to follow me."

Matthew 16:24

It is not enough to be convinced by the gospel intellectually and moved by the Spirit experientially. You must also die to self completely.

Pete Greig[5]

WHEN YOU HEAR THE WORD 'grit', what do you think of? Maybe sand or the salty stuff the Council spreads on the roads in the winter. Sand on the beach is great, but have you ever had sand in your bed or your mouth? It's highly unpleasant. Nobody wants sand where it doesn't belong, but there is a kind of grit that every Christian should have in their lives – spiritual grit.

Spiritual grit gives us traction on our road of discipleship. When the apostle Paul speaks about the Christian life, he associates it with things like being a soldier and being a runner in a race. Training in both fields is never easy; they require absolute commitment and strict training. The enduring commitment, however hard the challenges, is the grit that keeps the soldier soldiering on and the runner running to win. The glorious results of dedicated training are worth the painful efforts of the soldier and runner. Spiritual grit is about dying to self. Our flesh cries out for comfort and ease, but the Spirit calls us to greater things that comfort and ease will never know.

Something which knocks many new Christians for six concerning discipleship is discovering that Jesus means what he said when he offered, "If anyone wants to follow me, he must say no to himself. He must pick up his cross and follow me" (Matthew 24:16, NIRV). Jesus was committed to doing his Father's business. That business was to heal the sick, raise the dead and preach the good news to the poor and dispossessed. Looking good so far, but tacked onto that list was the bombshell he dropped on his unsuspecting disciples: "The Son of Man must suffer many things ... and be killed and be raised up on the third day" (Luke 9:22, NASB). The fact Jesus would have to suffer and die was too bitter a pill for the disciples to swallow. Jesus' disciple Peter didn't think much of it, that's for sure. He must have reasoned that if Jesus wasn't going to be spared hardship and suffering, then, as a close follower of Jesus, neither would he. Peter rebuked him concerning his statement about suffering and being killed, but Jesus' mind was made up. He was about his Father's business and if that business included dying on a cross, then so be it.

John Piper rightly states:

> The answer of the whole New Testament is this: the surprise about *Jesus the Messiah* is that he came to live a life of sacrificial, dying service before he comes a second time to reign in glory. And the surprise about *discipleship* is that it demands a life of sacrificial, dying service before we can reign with Christ in glory.[6]

Jesus was in it for the long haul, and he expects us to do the same – each one of us continuing faithfully on life's journey carrying our own cross of self-denial which will lead us to the reigning with Christ in glory bit, but not before we get on with carrying our personal cross of self-denial.

Spiritual grit is, in part, about dying to self. At first glance, this appears a very grim prospect – death. It is so final, but then death in God's Kingdom is very different from death as most would understand it on this spinning ball of dirt we call earth. When I was in primary school, we experimented with seeds and planted little beans inside clear plastic cups. Putting them into the dark potting soil, we saw nothing happen for days, but then they started to sprout, pushing a little taproot downwards and then a spindly green stalk upwards. It wasn't long before they were stretching out their waxy leaves over the school windowsill. Those little seeds had to 'die' in order to discover new life. It must be very comfortable to be a clean seed in a dry packet with a pretty picture on the front. What is not so nice is to be unceremoniously pressed into dank soil.

The fantastic news is that dying to self is not the end of the story. Jesus does call us to come and die, but only so that we can live; not for ourselves but for him. Elisabeth Elliot explains it well:

> We are not meant to die merely in order to be dead. God could not want that for the creatures to whom He has given the breath of life. We die in order to live.[7]

So what does dying to live look like? Each of us has desires and aspirations. Sometimes they are good for us, and other times they are not. They may include having sex outside of marriage, going out with the first person who happens to show any interest in us, or dabbling with taking illegal substances. How do we know what is right for us? We might be certain we know, but do we? I might think that my plan to put a flat-pack wardrobe together is better than the plan that is included in the packaging, but what happens when I do it my way? It might look perfectly fine when I have finished assembling it so speedily, but what about those extra screws and bolts that are left over when I stand back and look at my 'finished' wardrobe? Do I throw them away? Are they necessary? I will find out soon enough if I try to move it and find that it falls apart.

If we believe God is our creator, isn't it best that we look to him for instruction in how to live our lives? There will be times when his 'instructions' appear to go against the grain of what we want to do.

Iman is a member of our congregation and a gifted worship leader in our church. In her testimony, she shares something which really demonstrates why it is important for us to let God guide our steps instead of us deciding which way we want to go.

> I had been to all sorts of churches over my life and I remember enjoying one to the point of deciding to accept Jesus into my heart; I was eight or nine. It seemed reasonable that if I became a Christian, God would then look after me. I soon found that difficult things happened and God didn't do what I thought he should do for me. I decided that God would get no part of my life since he hadn't been there when I needed him. He hadn't stopped my dad from abusing my mother or trying to ship me off to Lebanon to marry my cousin. He wasn't there when I sobbed till the tears wouldn't come at having to leave everything

I knew and move from place to place to escape, or when I left everything I loved in Nigeria to move to a foreign land to escape my dad's grasp. He wasn't there when I prayed and prayed that he would heal my mum from sickle cell anaemia as she struggled to work and look after three children on her own in London. He didn't heal my granddad who always had my mum's back and would have protected us from the whole thing in the first place had he been around to stop my dad from being so abusive. My mum was adamant that God had a hand in everything and had looked after us through it all and she often called God her strength but all I could see was pain and struggle, so no, I had no space for God in my life. I spent a lot of energy ignoring his existence especially whenever I caught myself crying out to him in the middle of pain, fear or anxiety.

It was October 2007 and we had just moved into the neighbourhood, regeneration Church was just around the corner. I had walked past it twice or so and had stopped, transfixed by how colourful and vibrant it looked but I didn't let myself linger long … It was just a church, I wouldn't be fooled by the packaging.

During that last Sunday in October my mum announced that she would like me to come with her to church that evening. I scoffed at her. She had been there the week before, and was certain that I would enjoy it. I groaned and tried to get my visiting friend to weigh in on how ridiculous Mum was being. My mum was still adamant that I needed to go. She said, "I'm so sure you're meant to go there today that if you come, I promise I'll never ask you to go to church ever again." It was like music to my ears and I took her up on her offer before she had a chance to take it back, making sure to point out that my friend bore witness to the exchange. I convinced this friend to come along and joked about her being the one to save me should the church try to brainwash me. For the first time that I could remember I was very excited to go to church. The thought of never hearing some dull person tell me what I should, and shouldn't do, while asking for my money, and telling me that my sin was why my life sucked, was bliss.

As I walked in I was stunned at how young most people were and that it didn't seem like they were dragged along. People – about my age, looking like they WANTED to be in church. Everyone was friendly and welcoming but I made sure to sit right at the back for a quick escape at the end. The music was nice, the sermon seemed interesting enough; nothing seemed as dull as I expected and I almost felt sad that I would never return. Towards the end of the sermon a girl got up to share what God had done for her during a summer festival she attended. I found it unbelievable! Here was a girl who had very similar experiences in her childhood and a non-existent relationship with her dad, sharing how God was her Father and how loved she was. A part of me was angry at how happy she seemed – I was jealous. I remember thinking "I want what she has" and in that moment I felt this wave of something indescribable wash over me. I realised I was crying but didn't understand why. I looked at my confused friend and exclaimed, "I need to go talk to her." As she stood at the front offering to pray for people I walked over to her as fast as my feet could carry me, sobbing all the way. I just knew it was possible to have what she had. I felt it in my core that God was here and he wanted to show me how to know him and I decided to choose him then and there – I couldn't risk missing it. I could barely speak and half mumbled a request to be prayed for. I cried all through the prayer and didn't even notice the service had ended. I felt so light, so free and alive. Suddenly I had hope and a deep sense of joy, everything else seemed so unimportant. I returned to my friend beaming and told her she did a terrible job of stopping me from being sucked in. She said she had tried but it seemed like nothing could keep me back, it was like I was being pulled forward.

As I write this nearly nine years later, I am still amazed at how God knows when the perfect moment is to break in and reveal himself or his work. Suddenly I could see he was always present, always protecting and always providing. One of the most incredible things I noted from that day was how one act can change the course of a life. That girl shared her testimony for the first and ONLY time on that particular evening.

I cannot imagine how different my life would be had my mum not trusted what the Holy Spirit clearly impressed on her that day. I had plans of what I wanted to do and who I wanted to be, and I thought they would lead me to a life of joy and peace, but how wrong I was. God instead gave me more than I ever thought I could have.

It hasn't been an easy process. Through discipleship, I learned that although I opened my heart to God, I had to keep choosing to stay open and obedient. Early on, I prayed that God would reveal anything in the way of my getting closer to him and he opened up memories of childhood sexual abuse and began a process of working through the pain of memories and the effects it had on me. I had to decide again to either choose my way or to choose God's and forgive as I had been forgiven. More than my initial feeling that pulled me to him, I learned that following God meant wilfully choosing his way. Being in a church serious about discipleship helped me realise I couldn't just stay an angry, entitled, jealous and standoffish person, I had to lay down whatever God asked me to before I could receive all he wanted and still wants to pour in. There were days when it came easily because I could see exactly why I had to change; other times I found it so hard to change. I remember being so angry at not having my way I stormed out of the church band rehearsal but had to come back when the conviction of what I had done hit me hard.

I am so grateful for all of the grace God and my leaders have shown me over the years and continue to show me. I am unrecognisable, yet I know this is barely the beginning. As challenging as following Jesus can be, I have not regretted my decision to follow Jesus or to be discipled even when it is challenging.

I got healing from all of the pain of the past and received hope, joy, peace, a loving and supporting community, and later on a husband as well.

God continues to guide me through things I couldn't navigate through if I tried. Now I'm sure to let him lead me even through the things I think I could do on my own. I am ecstatic he didn't let me follow my own selfish plans for my life.

When we allow God to totally have his way in our lives like Iman did, we experience the joy of obedience and the reward that surrender to his lordship brings.

Many years ago, I experienced a long season of unemployment. I was too particular about what kinds of work I would and would not do. The economy was not going well and unemployment was high. I was talking to the greengrocer in our little village about my dilemma. She commented there were plenty of jobs working in care homes with elderly people. I replied matter of factly that I "wasn't interested in that sort of employment"– changing bedpans wasn't my idea of a successful career change. How arrogant and foolish of me. The apostle Paul plainly wrote, "Anyone who refuses to work should not eat" (2 Thessalonians 3:10). That is a straightforward statement. Who am I to say what I will and will not do, when the Bible makes it clear that refusing to work is wrong? Thankfully, the Holy Spirit convicted me of my off-beam attitude and I readily secured employment working with elderly people.

Something amazing came out of the simple act of saying yes to God's way that still echoes in my life today, for as a result of my getting a job working with elderly people, I discovered a compassion for them I didn't know I had. This led to me exploring the possibility of becoming a hospital chaplain, which steered me to candidate for ordained ministry. This is one of the positive results of me dying to my prejudice of not wanting to work with elderly people and being obedient to what God wanted me to do. If I didn't listen to God as he was speaking through the greengrocer – if I hadn't died to my own selfish desires – I would not have been in the right place to candidate for ordained ministry a year later. I would not have been spiritually mature enough and would not have had the necessary clarity to hear from God. In the year that followed, I learned a lot about dying to my selfish ambitions and putting God first.

Doing what God wants instead of what we want is dying to self. We place God's desires for us above our own. This is where true freedom begins. The devil will try to tell you freedom means not having to listen to or even believe in God, but he is a liar. Karl Rahner offers the following simple, but profound truth:

> How often I have found that we grow to maturity not by doing what we like, but by doing what we should. How true it is that not every 'should' is a compulsion, and not every 'like' is a high morality and true freedom.[8]

Karl Rahner

Doing what we should, even when we don't want to, is achieved by applying the 'grit' of dying to self to our journey. Grit in the wrong place is unhelpful and uncomfortable. Like sand in your shoe, it serves no useful purpose, but in the right place it gives us the traction we need on the sometimes-slippery road of life.

When my younger brother, John, and I were boys, we were travelling in the back seat of my grandfather's faded blue '63 Chevrolet Biscayne down the dirt road that ran away from our small farm. The road was heavily covered with snow and the conditions were far from ideal for driving. I didn't help the situation by mercilessly teasing my brother in the back seat. This caused a distraction for Pop-Pop; he turned around to tell us to stop fighting. The greatest problem at that moment was not our arguing but that he wasn't looking where he was going. John and I, however, saw clearly that the road ahead took a sharp right, and we didn't stand any chance of making the bend, given the trajectory and speed in which we were travelling.

In unison John and I pointed at the oncoming cataclysm and shouted, "Pop-Pop!" He slammed on the brakes, which didn't help avoid the calamity at all. We soon found ourselves sliding off the road spectacularly into a snow bank with the car bonnet nicely resting under the branches of a low-hanging tree. Silence. An awkward moment. Then Pop-Pop tried reversing the car out of the snow bank, to no avail. Every rev of the engine sent the rear wheels rotating nicely, spitting out snow like an icy Catherine Wheel, but that was getting us nowhere except closer to the ground. We were hopelessly stuck, or so we thought, until a couple in a car happened to pass by. It was rather handy that they had a shovel and some grit with them.

The most heartening thing to know is that Jesus is well aware of our struggles on the sometimes treacherous road of life we travel, and that he cares deeply. Brennan Manning gives a clear assessment of Jesus' understanding of what the cost of discipleship means for us:

> When Jesus said, "Come to me, all you who labour and are heavy burdened," He assumed we would grow weary, discouraged, and disheartened along the way. These words are a touching testimony to the genuine humanness of Jesus. He had no romantic notion of the cost of discipleship. He knew that following Him was as unsentimental as duty, as demanding as love.[9]

Jesus' call of duty for us to come and die, to kill our earthly desires on the road waymarked with suffering, is not as bad as it looks. In fact, it is very good news. What the apostle Paul wrote to the Romans is great news for every believer:

> But if the Spirit of Him who raised Jesus from the dead dwells in you, He who raised Christ Jesus from the dead will also give life to your mortal bodies through His Spirit who dwells in you.

> Romans 8:11 (NASB)

We should never lose sight of the fact that the journey of discipleship will mean numerous 'deaths' for us throughout our lives. There will be the necessary deaths to our secret sins, jealousies, prideful attitudes, vanities and wilful lusts. We don't have to worry about those obligatory deaths, though, for the one who was tortured, crucified, killed and buried for the sake of us was raised to life that we might receive eternal life through him. The great news is that the living starts now. Dying to self only means there will be more of the life of Jesus in us. Isn't that more than a fair exchange?

So we have good reason to keep going and not give up. Many people try to live a sold-out life for God and if the results aren't immediate, they give up and walk away from Christianity as if it is something of little consequence. As disciples of Jesus, we are called to keep going, no matter how bleak the outlook is. Consider this:

> A southern writer named John Kennedy Toole wrote a comic novel about life in New Orleans called *A Confederacy of Dunces*. It was so persistently rejected by publishers that he eventually committed suicide. This was back in 1969. His mother refused to give up in her efforts to get the book published. She sent it out and got it back, rejected, repeatedly. At last she got the patronage of Walker Percy, who got it accepted by the Louisiana University State Press, and in 1981 it won the Pulitzer Prize for fiction.[10]

If only John hadn't given up when those rejection letters fell like dirty confetti on his doormat. It is sad that he never lived to see the awesome reward of his labours. What a salient lesson this is for us as we march towards the goal of becoming more like Jesus. This is an objective far greater than merely getting a book published.

See how Paul cheered the Galatians on with these words:

> And let us not get tired of doing what is right, for after a while we will reap a harvest of blessing if we don't get discouraged and give up.
>
> Galatians 6:9 (TLB)

In spite of the difficulties the Galatians faced, Paul encouraged them to keep on doing what was right, even though they were probably near to being worn out. In the early years of numerical growth at regen, there were people in the area accusing Ruth and me of stealing young people from other churches. It was hard for us to hear this kind of criticism, since the majority of the young people we had coming along had no church background at all. It felt so unfair to be labelled "sheep stealers" when all we wanted to do was see young people come to faith in Jesus.

Instead of fighting back and getting into a slanging match with these people, we just kept on with what God was calling us to do at regen. We determined we were not going to go out of our way to defend ourselves. Sometimes this meant sitting in meetings with other church representatives and quietly listening while slanderous accusations were made against us. I eventually asked one of our greatest critics if he would help me with some spiritual guidance. He was somewhat surprised by my request, but I think it helped him to understand me more and it killed the pride in me that said I didn't need his wisdom. Our responses to our enemies didn't come easily, but we knew it was what God wanted us to do, however uncomfortable it may have been for us.

Doing what is right by God's standards may feel as though it is killing our pride and sense of self-preservation, but that is OK. Obedient discipline and dying to self is the grit that keeps us moving forward in faith. This is true grit; this is holy grit.

It is absolutely essential that we do our best as followers of Jesus, sure, there is abundant grace available for every disciple, but the old Welsh preacher put it well when he said, "You supply the grit and God will supply the grace."[11] When we experience the remarkable resurrection life of Christ in our daily walk with him, we appreciate that spiritual grit isn't such bad stuff after all.

THREE

INTERDEPENDENCE

Paul uses the term "one another", I think it's 34 times in his letters, let alone what's in Hebrews and the gospels and the letters of John. We need to be a community that supports one another and above all supports one another in the sort of habits that form Christian character.

Bishop Graham Cray[12]

Discipleship is a call to me, but it is a journey of "we".

Michael Spencer[13]

I N AN AGE THAT HIGHLY VALUES personal independence, the Church speaks of something better – interdependence. We are members of a body, the body of Christ (1 Corinthians 12:12–27). God expects us to interconnect with one another like a human body is interconnected with its members. There will be times when we would really prefer to go it alone, but God in his wisdom gives us interdependence as a blessing. There is an old African proverb that says, "It takes a village to raise a child." In a similar way, it takes a church to raise a Christian.

> But encourage one another daily, as long as it is called "Today," so that none of you may be hardened by sin's deceitfulness.
>
> Hebrews 3:13 (NIV)

When we are strong in faith, we are able to help members who may be struggling. When we are feeling weak and without hope, our brothers and sisters in Christ can lift us up. This works not only in spiritual ways, but in practical ways as well. A few years ago, I had a terrible infection. I was sitting at my desk trying to work, but it was becoming impossible to do anything. With my head heavily resting in my hands, I told Ruth I was feeling incredibly tired. She suggested I go lie down for a while and so I did, non-stop for six weeks. The diagnosis was viral labyrinthitis. It was a terrible and frightening experience. I had unrelenting nausea and vomiting and terrible vertigo. Walking became virtually impossible. If I wanted to go from one room to the next, I had to hold onto furniture and support myself against walls to get anywhere.

Eventually, I spent a week in hospital due to becoming so helplessly weak and incapacitated. During that time, the wonderful people at regen and another church looked after me very well. Some cooked meals and visited me in hospital, others took me out for drives in their car when I was feeling a bit better and could stand the sensation of movement. One Sunday I wanted to go to church so much, but I wasn't able to cross the street by myself to get to it. A young man from our congregation came to my house and supported me by holding me up as I stumbled like a drunkard to the church. Little did I know then that later that summer I would be helping Michael through one of the darkest times of his life.

Michael had a sore throat for a couple of weeks, that was all – or so it seemed. Then one Monday morning, he woke up and found he could not stand up. As that dark week progressed, he gradually lost sensation further and further up his body. The paralysis travelled rapidly up his spine, leaving him without feeling up to his chest. His eyesight began to fail too. The doctors were not even confident that he was going to make it. I had made a full recovery by then, which was a blessing since I was able to sit by Michael's bed and pray for him and, when he was too weak to lift a spoon, I fed him his dinner. This is how the Church works as a body. We support one another in our times of weakness and strength in both physical and spiritual ways.

Ruth has helped me to see irritating things about myself that I have been completely blind. Sometimes I would prefer to continue on carelessly through life with my faults firmly in tow, but I have come to realise that if I want to grow, if I want to be a great husband to Ruth, I will have to acknowledge my shortcomings and irksome behaviours and work to eradicate their hold on me.

Ruth recently pointed out that if I disagree about something with my son Stephen, I will argue with him childishly. I didn't want to hear that, but it was something my immature self needed to hear. Then there was the time a young man on our leadership team told me I always thought my ideas were best. At first, I did not fully accept his insight to be valid, but upon reflection I came to realise there was truth in what he said. We all need friends who will hold a mirror to our face in order that we may see and understand ourselves clearly, even if it makes us feel uncomfortable.

Removing faults and sinful habits we have developed over a lifetime isn't easy, but we can kick them into the long grass with the help of loving family and friends who speak honestly into our lives. Interdependence is essential in our journey of discipleship. A simple proverb illustrates this point well:

> As iron sharpens iron, so one person sharpens another.

> Proverbs 27:17 (NIVUK)

Jack is a young man in our church who agreed to share his story of how he has been changed by this principle:

I grew up in a Christian home and became a Christian at an early age, but never really thought about the importance of interdependence because, as far as I was aware, everyone was united all the time. However, as I matured in my faith and grew up as a person, I noticed that this isn't human nature, nor was it as widely practised as I would have hoped. People held grudges, they gossiped, cliques were established. This eventually led to me the darkest times in my life, and drew me away from God, but not from the promises I knew to be true: that he loved me, and that he wasn't going to leave me there. I went into depression for two and a half years. After two years, I ended up self-harming and eventually got suicidal. And all through this I didn't have anyone to talk to about it. I remembered something I heard at another church about how important it is through tough times to have someone there to help you. Throughout this time, I felt God was telling me to try other churches, so I tried a few but couldn't find the right one. Then I found regeneration, a church where I could feel the loving, caring atmosphere from the outset. As I walked through the doors at regen for the first time, God took it all away. I could physically feel the weight being lifted from my shoulders. Since then, regen has taught me the importance of interdependence, how we need to hold each other up in faith, how accountability can encourage you when the enemy attacks, and the true meaning of a church family. If it wasn't for the community at regen, I wouldn't be as free as I am today. God uses interdependence for his glory!

Living this way means not only loving people you like, but also loving people who annoy you. It means not just wanting unity when you feel like it, but knowing you need to seek it all the more when you feel isolated. It means not judging others by our standards but seeing them through God's eyes.

This is the journey that I am on at the moment. God is teaching me not to be too proud. To ask for help when I need it, because I now have people around me who genuinely care for me. He's teaching me that my identity is not found in what others think of me, but in God and God alone. He's teaching me that I can't do life by myself, I need people to speak into my life; I need challenge, and encouragement. He's teaching me that other people can help me draw nearer to him.

Jack has learned that God's glorious plan for us all is that we support one another selflessly as the body of Christ. The apostle Paul encouraged the Romans to do just that:

> We who are strong in faith should help the weak with their weaknesses, and not please only ourselves. Let each of us please our neighbours for their good, to help them be stronger in faith.

> Romans 15:1–2

Each of us has our own unique set of strengths and weaknesses, leaving us plenty of scope to be helpful to people who are weaker in an area where we are strong. When we are weak there will be someone else who is stronger and can help lift us up to where we should be. Thank God for the body of Christ. We can't help others or ourselves to make it to our goal without the help of the Holy Spirit. I'm going to explore this wonderful gift in the next chapter.

FOUR

IT'S DYNAMITE!

But when the Holy Spirit comes to you, you will receive power. You will be my witnesses – in Jerusalem, in all of Judea, in Samaria, and in every part of the world.

Jesus, Acts 1:8

With God's power working in us, God can do much, much more than anything we can ask or imagine.

Ephesians 3:20

EVERY NEW BELIEVER NEEDS TO KNOW that once they commit their lives to Christ, they should expect that God will ask them to do things that are deemed impossible in their natural human state. That is how God works. He does this to demonstrate, to ourselves and others, that the age of miracles is not past. He works in impossible situations to make them possible by the power of the Holy Spirit at work in lives surrendered to his will.

31

The Holy Spirit's power is the key to doing what is deemed impossible. To get anything moving or working, power is required. When we read about Jesus delivering the good news to his disciples and telling them that they were going to receive power from the Holy Spirit, the Greek word for power used is *dunamis*. That is where the word 'dynamite' comes from. Dynamite can do impressive things, such as blast tunnels through rock-solid mountains.

I had a friend who was in the United States Army Special Forces, known as the Green Berets, who somehow managed to smuggle out a training exercise 'bomb' which, he boasted to me, was equal in power to one-fifth a stick of dynamite.[1] He asked if I would like him to set it off in our garden. Being twelve years old at the time, I was like, "Heck yeah!" We moved swiftly to the front porch of my house after he set it off. At first, there was a tremendously loud whistling sound mimicking a bomb falling out of the sky (this was really spectacular in itself), followed by a tremendous explosion like I never heard before or since, quickly followed by a forceful wall of air that came at us with magnificent speed in one mighty sonic wave. The windows of the house rattled and shook. I was surprised they hadn't all broken. The neighbour who lived across the street called my mum immediately after the explosion. To say she was "not happy" would be an understatement. I

---

1   Whether this is true or not I don't know but it got my attention straightaway.

experienced a little of what dynamite was like that day, and it gave me a greater appreciation of its power.

Do we appreciate the power the Spirit has given us? Supernatural dynamite power is at our disposal whenever we need it. When we face mountains of difficulty that block the way ahead, we need the Spirit's dynamite power. When roots of sin, like lust, self-harming, or other addictive behaviours won't budge, the Holy Spirit's power will eliminate them. When the devil displays lies like giant billboards in our path, seeking to intimidate us on our discipleship journey, holy dynamite power will blast them down.

Jesus said:

> I have given you authority to trample on snakes and scorpions and to overcome all the power of the enemy; nothing will harm you.
>
> Luke 10:19 (NIVUK)

This is great news from the lips of Jesus, but if we don't appropriate them into our lives, we might as well admit defeat. However, as the writer to the Hebrews says:

> But we are not like those who turn away from God to their own destruction. We are the faithful ones, whose souls will be saved.
>
> Hebrews 10:39 (NLT)

It is soul-destroying to be given a demanding task but not have the proper tools and instructions to carry it out. The great news is that the Holy Spirit not only gives power, he also gives wisdom to know how to live as a power-filled overcomer in a broken world. Here's what the apostle Paul had to say about the Holy Spirit's ability to give us wisdom:

> And we have received God's Spirit (not the world's spirit), so we can know the wonderful things God has freely given us. When we tell you these things, we do not use words that come from human wisdom. Instead, we speak words given to us by the Spirit, using the Spirit's words to explain spiritual truths. But people who aren't spiritual can't receive these truths from God's Spirit. It all sounds foolish to them and they can't understand it, for only those who are spiritual can understand what the Spirit means.
>
> 1 Corinthians 2:12–14 (NLT)

It is impossible to live a godly life without the Holy Spirit's wisdom and power. People who try to live without them either end up like legalistic fruitcakes on escalators to outer space, or hyper-spiritual fanatics who make a lot of noise but don't do anything worthwhile for God's Kingdom.

So what does this look like in real life? How does the Spirit's power help a young man overcome a lustful addiction to pornography, or a woman break free of the power of gambling or alcoholism? In Romans, the apostle Paul explains that we are dead to sin:

> For we know that our old self was crucified
> with him so that the body ruled by sin
> might be done away with, that we should no
> longer be slaves to sin – because anyone who
> has died has been set free from sin. Now if
> we died with Christ, we believe that we will
> also live with him. For we know that since
> Christ was raised from the dead, he cannot
> die again; death no longer has mastery over
> him. The death he died, he died to sin once
> for all; but the life he lives, he lives to God.
> In the same way, count yourselves dead to
> sin but alive to God in Christ Jesus.

Romans 6:6–11 (NIV)

Sin doesn't have power over us any more than a person could have power over something that is dead. You can't ride a dead horse; you can't make it gallop, jump over fences, or even make it stand up. It is dead. In the same way, when we become Christians we are no longer under the control or power of sin. We have become dead to it by being buried with Christ. Sin cannot control us unless we give in to it. One of the greatest things we can know in this life is that we have the power to say "no" to sin. Addictions are powerful, but the power of the Spirit is greater than any binding addiction. Sometimes people can be set free from an addiction immediately, but there can be a process involved which brings freedom over time as past sins are dealt with and any lingering bitter attitudes towards others are resolved.

Issues of unforgiveness we might have with people who have hurt us will need addressing. Whatever mountain of difficulty you may face, it is worth noting that there is nothing, absolutely nothing, greater than the power of the Holy Spirit's power to get rid of mountains that seem to block the way to right living. This truth should give us great confidence when we are tempted to believe Satan's lies that tell us we are powerless to do anything except to sin.

There is a defensive role the Spirit plays in our lives, but there is also an offensive role we are expected to play a part in. Jesus sends us out to make a difference in the world. In the Bible, our presence on earth is compared to salt and to light – the salt in the world to act as a preservative and the light to dispel evil darkness. In God's mission, we are called to break down injustice and suffering wherever we find it. We may feel ill-equipped in this mission, but the fact remains that we are highly equipped by the Spirit's power at work in us. We really need to understand that the Spirit's power is for more than merely helping us resist the devil's lies and schemes. We equally have the power of the Spirit to transform culture. Our God-given mission is to literally change the world with the good news of Jesus Christ.

Nicky Gumbel, the vicar of a lively and mission-orientated church, remarked:

> In every generation, the world is changed by a few people, who stand for something, do not fear unpopularity and dare to make a difference.[14]

You can be one of those people if you accept the challenge. Dare to make a difference by the power of the Spirit living powerfully in you. Dare to share your faith in Jesus Christ with anyone who will listen to you. Dare to challenge someone else to make a difference too. Determine that today will be different than all the other days that have gone before. But before you set off on this great adventure – if you haven't already – there is more we need to look at. Another essential ingredient for successful living is love. We should never do the work God has called us to do without it.

FIVE

IT'S ALL ABOUT THE LOVE

Your love for one another will prove to the world
that you are my disciples.

Jesus, John 13:35 (NLT)

If I speak in the tongues of men or of angels, but do
not have love, I am only a resounding gong or a
clanging cymbal. If I have the gift of prophecy and can
fathom all mysteries and all knowledge, and if I have
a faith that can move mountains, but do not have
love, I am nothing. If I give all I possess to the poor
and give over my body to hardship that I may boast,
but do not have love, I gain nothing. Love is patient,
love is kind. It does not envy, it does not boast, it is
not proud. It does not dishonour others, it is not self-
seeking, it is not easily angered, it keeps no record of
wrongs. Love does not delight in evil but rejoices with
the truth. It always protects, always trusts, always
hopes, always perseveres. Love never fails.

1 Corinthians 13:1–8 (NIV)

> Love is friendship that has caught fire. It is quiet understanding, mutual confidence, sharing and forgiving. It is loyalty through good and bad times. It settles for less than perfection and makes allowances for human weaknesses.
>
> Ann Landers[15]

Let's start with the bottom line: if we don't have love, we are nothing. Strong words? Yeah, but let's face it, they're true. Without love we are nothing and we gain nothing. Think about the most unloving person you know (hopefully it's not you). How do you feel when you are around that person? Do you hate, pity, or love them? When I am tempted to do the first two towards the most unloving person I know, the Holy Spirit reminds me that God's love for them is equal to his love for me. That piercing revelation penetrates my arrogant heart like a hot knife through butter.

Now think about this: Who is the most loving person you know? Can you imagine God loves you as much as he does them? Oh yes, he loves us all the same. Let that sink down deep into your heart. He loves you as much as the most worthy person you can think of or could imagine. He will always love you. With that kind of knowledge about yourself, there should be no room for feelings of unworthiness or self-contempt, only a growing awareness that your future is looking tremendously bright. Not only do you have the power of the Holy Spirit in you, but you also have the unconditional love of the Father shining down on you. Consider this:

> And I am convinced that nothing can ever separate us from God's love. Neither death nor life, neither angels nor demons, neither our fears for today nor our worries about tomorrow—not even the powers of hell can separate us from God's love. No power in the sky above or in the earth below—indeed, nothing in all creation will ever be able to separate us from the love of God that is revealed in Christ Jesus our Lord.
>
> Romans 8:38–39 (NLT)

Now that is something to celebrate. When we are confident in God's love, we can risk loving others no matter what they throw at us. They say that love is a four-letter word spelt r-i-s-k. If we are to love as Christ loved us, we are going to risk having that love rejected or abused, but that is OK because God has our back all the time. He is watching over us with his unconditional love that never tires or runs out.

It had to be the great love of Jesus that first attracted his disciples to follow him in the first place. It's hard to imagine them wanting to follow a harsh and unloving disciplinarian who would only teach them the bald facts of what it meant to live a holy life. In those three incredible years they did follow Christ, his teaching and demonstrations of love won them over in such a way that they were willing to follow him despite the gritty realities of discipleship and the risks involved. There were times when it would have been far easier for them to pack it all in and say, "Enough is enough." The attraction to Christ was far more than his brilliant teaching; we know this because he lived and spoke words of life. Look at what his closest disciple had to say about him: "In him there was life, and that life was the light of all people" (John 1:4).

One of my favourite passages of Scripture is the account of Jesus delivering some pretty hard teaching to his followers; kind of like the gritty stuff I was talking about in the chapter about true grit. He is telling them about the real cost of discipleship without pulling any punches. Here's what happens:

> After Jesus said this, many of his followers left him and stopped following him. Jesus asked the twelve followers, "Do you want to leave, too?" Simon Peter answered him, "Lord, who would we go to? You have the words that give eternal life. We believe and know that you are the Holy One from God."

> John 6:66-69

That speaks volumes to me. The disciples are willing to give up everything, even though they don't understand all that Jesus is saying to them, despite knowing the obvious, that hard times lie ahead. They know and appreciate that Jesus has words of life; there is nothing else, no one else who can satisfy their desire for more of God and the knowledge of his love.

So what does God expect us to do with his love? Share it out and spread it around because there is plenty more where that came from. Be a strong-hearted, extravagant lover to this world. Generously dish it out, not with teaspoons, but with dump trucks, and make sure that it's not just to people you know but to those you don't. When you pass people on the street say a cheerful, "Hello!" Who cares if they don't return the greeting? You cannot be diminished in any way by their lack of response. In fact, by loving others this way, the love of God grows a little bit more in your heart. When you give to others from a heart of love, God will multiply it back to you in spades. That is just what he is like, this almighty, loving God of ours. He wants us to love everyone with his wild, unrelenting love. He wants us to love in such a way that people in the world are compelled to say, "Wow! This love is incredible!"

I wish I could say that in every situation I face that I am always loving, but that would be an absurd lie. Only this morning, I acted in an unloving way. One of my sons came to our home and was merely asking me where his door key was. When I said, "Hanging up" it wasn't enough information for him, so he asked me again, to which I merely repeated what I said and pointed in the general direction of where the key was, which was by no means a loving response. What did I do immediately after my rude reply? I came into my office to work on this chapter on love.

As you can see, I have a long way to go in the love department. I knew it was useless for me to work on this chapter when I was being such a hypocrite. I went back and made things right with my son. I apologised for my unloving behaviour and for being proud by not apologising straight away. There is no way around the truth that if I want to live in the security of God's love, I have to obey his law of love. I'm still learning.

Having established our identity in the Father's love as a safe foundation for our loving of others, we can now look at the things that hinder us from reaching our destination of becoming more like Jesus Christ.

SIX

ROADBLOCKS

This is what the LORD says.
He is the one who made a road through the sea
and a path through rough waters.

Isaiah 43:16

If you're trying to achieve, there will be roadblocks.
I've had them; everybody has had them. But obstacles
don't have to stop you. If you run into a wall, don't
turn around and give up. Figure out how to climb it,
go through it, or work around it.

Michael Jordan[16]

WHEN RUTH AND I SET OFF on a car journey, I like
to leave with ample time to "allow for eventuali-
ties". Ruth is happy to leave the house at the last possible
minute, which means we don't always get to where we
need to be on time. Inevitably, we come across roadblocks.

They appear in many shapes and sizes: car accidents, over-turned lorries, fires by the roadside, floods, roads closed for repair, fallen branches, bridges out of action – the list goes on. Ruth and I have experienced all of these. Sometimes there is nothing we can do but sit and wait, while at other times we find a way to get around them. It may require a long detour or getting out of the car and dragging a branch to the side of the road. Roadblocks are frustrating. Spiritual roadblocks are too, but when we know what kind of roadblocks we are dealing with, we will know how to get around them in the most effective way.

The great news is that no roadblock ever needs to stop us from moving forward in our spiritual journey. If we ask the Holy Spirit to be our guide, he can help remove blockages so that we can move on into the life that Jesus promised us. The following roadblocks are common to Christians who are endeavouring to be more like Jesus. It may seem daunting to have to deal with these, but take heart, the Holy Spirit can help you find your way over, around, or through each one.

PRIDE

> There are six things the LORD hates.
> There are seven things he cannot stand:
> a proud look …
>
> Proverbs 6:16–17

Number one on the Lord's list of things he hates is "a proud look". Taking this into consideration, we really have to get a handle on pride if we want to live lives that are pleasing to God.

Pride is insidious. Just when you think you have conquered the creeping smugness it brings, you warmly congratulate yourself for conquering it, only to realise you have become proud of not being proud. The battle with our pride can seem relentless.

I can confidently say from the outset that I have been guilty of pride as much as any other person. Pride of self has no limits. It defies human logic and reasoning. What do we have to be proud of when all we have is from God? Our talents, abilities, great looks – whatever we possess, all come from him.

I used to lead worship at regen. I wasn't very good at it; nevertheless, I became proud in leading on the stage. If I managed to hit all the high notes and keep in tune, I allowed pride to subtly worm its way into my heart. I battled against it for some time. It became so bad I just wanted to stop leading worship altogether so I wouldn't have to deal with the constant battle raging in my heart, but there was no one ready to take over from me. God had other plans. He intended that I continue leading worship until I could root the stubborn pride out of my life.

It was a battle; it was a hard-won battle. When I finally retired from leading worship, I was so happy because I was retiring for the right reason. I managed to tackle my pride by radical confession to Ruth – many times. I would tell her of my struggle, we would pray and I would get back on the stage with a new determination to let all my focus be on Jesus and not on myself and my efforts to sing well. Over the course of time, I was able to conquer my pride in worship-leading, which meant a great burden lifted off me.

Getting rid of pride should be a number one priority for any Christian. Being able to share my struggle with Ruth was so helpful for me in overcoming. I strongly encourage you to share your struggles against pride with an accountability partner. An accountability partner is someone who looks out for us, who will ask the hard questions we sometimes may avoid asking ourselves. Questions like: How is your prayer life? Are you taking enough time out of your busy schedule to recharge? How is your commitment to not getting drunk when you are out with friends? Whatever our particular issues are, questions like these help keep us on track with our commitment to following Jesus on the great road of discipleship.

It is not the role of the accountability partner to live our lives for us; rather, it is their job to be there for us; to share the journey of discipleship. Being accountable to another Christian helps to keep us on the right track and it helps them to know us better and pray for us more effectively. They won't think of us any less as we share our faults, struggles and failures. In fact, they will respect us more for being real. It's definitely a win-win situation. Humbling ourselves before one another is the antidote to pride and self-reliance.

> … And all of you should be very humble
> with each other.
> "God is against the proud,
> but he gives grace to the humble."
>
> 1 Peter 5:5

Letting go of our pride and taking on Christ's humility is one of the best things we can do for ourselves.

CHERRY-PICKING

> So Moses told the people, "You must be careful to obey all the commands of the Lord your God, following his instructions in every detail."
>
> Deuteronomy 5:32 (NLT)

> IT WAS A COMMON SAYING AMONG the Christians of the primitive church, "the soul and the body make a man; the spirit and discipline make a Christian:" implying that none could be real Christians without the help of Christian discipline. But if this be so, is it any wonder that we find so few Christians; for where is Christian discipline?
>
> John Wesley[17]

I mentioned earlier that one young man who left our church said, "It's not about us having to change, Jesus didn't ask us to do that, he did it all on the cross." That young man didn't understand that an essential part of Jesus' message of salvation was a demand to change.

God expects us to change, and he promised we would have the power to do so by the Holy Spirit in us. At times it may seem too hard to take the necessary steps to change, but it can be done. We shouldn't have a cavalier approach to what God has revealed to us in Scripture. The Bible is full of wonderful promises, but it is also full of commands. We cannot accept one without the other.

Consider the story of Sara, a woman who had experienced a great deal of unhappiness in her childhood. Poor choices in her life had made her circumstances very difficult. She wanted change. She prayed with people who counselled her. As they talked, the Holy Spirit gave her insight into the wrong reactions she had had to her parents' bad handling of her as a child. As she worked through the counselling session, she began to weep and pray that God would forgive her. Here's what happened next:

> … we prayed for Jesus to come and heal her. As together we waited on God the Holy Spirit gave her a clear picture of herself in a filthy room in which there was a bed crawling with insects. Sara said she felt very small and although she saw a bucket and mop there, she did not feel able to clean the room alone. We continued to wait on God. We were amazed at His words to her: "Some things I will do for you; some things we will

> do together and some things you will have to
> do on your own while I watch." Sara had
> heard the truth. Only she could do the
> repenting necessary ... God could not do
> that for her. Only He could forgive and heal
> her, she could not do that for herself. But
> only in co-operation with God would she be
> able to change her behaviour patterns.[18]

Sara could have presumed her problems were a result of her parents' bad parenting skills, consequently leaving her off the hook and free to behave as she wished. But the mature response for her was to knuckle down to the sometimes difficult process of change and transformation. Spiritual healing and maturity for Sara required her to do some things for herself.

There is a lesson for all of us in Sara's story. God expects us to come under the discipline of obeying what the Bible commands. We cannot presume upon God and cherry-pick the scriptures to suit whatever whim or desire we may have. If we want to be mature in Christ, we will have to be mature in our understanding of what God is requiring from us. Jesus expected his followers to change – he called them to repentance and obedience, and he calls us to the same.

In Matthew's Gospel there is an account of Jesus being severely tempted by the devil. He used his usual dirty tricks to try to get Jesus to forfeit his power by sinning. After the temptation account, we read that Jesus travelled to Capernaum. What are his first recorded words to the Caperneans after this severe test?

> "The time has come," he said. "The kingdom of God has come near. Repent and believe the good news!"

Mark 1:15 (NIV)

Jesus didn't say, "Hey, chaps, I've had a frightful struggle with the devil and I kicked some butt so don't worry about him." No, he said, "Change your hearts and lives, because the kingdom of heaven is near." Jesus was doing his part to bring in a new Kingdom, but he expected others to have to do things as well, which meant people would have to start changing the way they lived their lives. Jesus does things for us like giving us a new start by forgiving us for the wrong we have done and setting us on the right road. We are responsible for living the life he calls us to. We do this as individuals, but we also do this with one another. The Bible makes it clear that we have a part to play. There is no room for selectivity in God's economy.

I discovered this in a period in my life where I found my times of prayer hard going. I slacked a bit and thought God would have me covered. I figured I could coast for a while. How wrong I was. I lost ground in my devotional time with God and it took me some time to build it up again.

As Christians, we need to rediscover the great benefits of the spiritual disciplines. Dallas Willard, in *The Spirit of the Disciplines[19]*, and Richard Foster, in *Celebration of Discipline[20]*, have assembled a list of spiritual disciplines and practices they believe were modelled in the life of Christ. The disciplines are ordered into two categories: the disciplines of abstinence and the disciplines of activity.

Disciplines of letting go

These practices allow us to relinquish something in order to gain something new. Through the disciplines we withdraw from busyness in ministry, family life, social activities and work.

Solitude – Spend time alone to be with God. Find a quiet place to be alone with the Lord for a period. Use the Bible as a source to reenergise friendship with God.

Silence – Remove noisy distractions to hear from God. Find a quiet place away from noise to hear from God. Write your thoughts and impressions as God speaks to your heart. Silence can occur even in the centre of noise and distraction. But you have to focus your attention on your soul. This could mean talking less or talking only when necessary. And it could mean putting down an iPad or game console, and turning off the television.

Fasting – Skip a meal(s) to find greater nourishment from God. Choose a period of time to go without food. Feel the pain of having an empty stomach and depend on God to fill you with his grace.

Frugality – Learn to live with less money and still meet your basic needs. Before buying something new, choose to go without or pick a less expensive alternative that will serve your basic needs. Live a simple, focused life.

Chastity – Voluntarily choose to abstain from marital sexual pleasures for a time to find higher fulfillment in God. Married couples may set aside time to go without sexual pleasures in order to experience a deeper relationship with the Lord in prayer.

Secrecy – Avoid self-promotion, practise serving God without others knowing. Give in secret. Serve 'behind the scenes' in a ministry that you know few will be aware of.

Sacrifice – Give of resources beyond what seems reasonable to remind you of your dependence on Christ. Choose to give your time or finances to the Lord beyond what you normally would.

Disciplines of activity

Dallas Willard writes, "The disciplines of abstinence must be counter-balanced and supplemented by disciplines of engagement (activity)."[21] It's choosing to participate in activities that nurture our souls and strengthen us for the race ahead.

Study – Spend time reading the Scriptures and meditating on its meaning and importance to your life. The Word nourishes us because it is our source of spiritual strength. Decide a time and a place to feed from the Bible regularly.

Worship – Offering praise and adoration to God. God's praise should continually be on our lips and in our thoughts. Read psalms, hymns, or spiritual songs, or sing to the Lord daily. Keep praise before you as you think of God's remarkable activities in your life.

Prayer – Talk to and listen to God about your relationship with him and about the concerns of others. Find time to pray to God without the distraction of people or things. Combine your prayer time with meditation on the Scriptures in order to focus on Christ.

Fellowship – Mutual care and ministry in the body of Christ. Meet regularly with other Christians to find ways to minister to others. Encourage one another to be better disciples of Jesus.

Confession – Regularly confess your sins to the Lord and other trusted individuals. As often as you are aware of sin in your life, confess it to the Lord and to those you may have offended.

Submission – Humble yourself before God and others while seeking accountability in relationships. Find faithful brothers or sisters in Christ who can lovingly hold you accountable for your actions and growth in Christ.[22]

If we let our guard down by choosing what parts of discipleship we will and will not do, we are only asking to be 'taken out' by the devil. Do we really want to allow ourselves to be something akin to the devil's chew toy? We shouldn't take anything for granted in God's Kingdom. God hasn't called us to a pick-and-mix religion – he calls us to something far more challenging and real than that. By embracing all that God has for us by way of the spiritual disciplines, we will enjoy a far more healthy spiritual diet than if we choose to cherry-pick our way through our Christian lives.

UNFORGIVENESS

To forgive is to set a prisoner free and discover that the prisoner was you.

Lewis B. Smedes[23]

Jesus said you are to love one another as I have loved you, a love that will possibly lead to the bloody, anguished gift of yourself, a love that forgives seven times seven, that keeps no record of wrong. This is the criterion, sole norm, the standard of discipleship in the New Israel of God.

Brennan Manning[24]

And forgive us our sins, as we forgive those who sin against us.

Jesus

Luke 11:4 (NLT)

I answered the phone in our hallway expecting to hear the voice of a friend or someone trying to sell me double glazing, but was piqued to discover it was Luke, a man I hadn't spoken to in years. He asked to speak to one of our friends. I said I would get her for him in as much of a monotone voice as I could muster, but inwardly I was seething, determined there was no way I was going to speak warmly to him. In my small-minded way, I was perpetuating what he had done to my family and me for several years.

Although I had forgiven him many times before for his cruel and bitter actions towards me and members of my family, I was aware that I was developing forgiveness fatigue. A seed of bitterness was taking root in my heart; I came to discover that I actually enjoyed harbouring and polishing it. I kept it like a black pearl, deep in the murky recess of my unforgiving heart.

Any forgiveness I had for Luke had long worn thin and the subtle but dangerous conclusion I had come to was that hate was the better option. Nothing ever changed in his attitude or relationship with others. He was as cold and calculating as ever in his drive to manipulate the people I loved. I had had enough; doing the right thing by forgiving was seemingly not achieving anything.

Not long after this phone call, my wife, Ruth, and I were walking along a river near a wonderful Christian retreat centre on the north Devon coast. She gently asked me if I had said anything to Luke when I answered his call. I was surprised and a little annoyed to be blindsided by such a direct question. I didn't think Ruth could possibly know what was going on inside my unforgiving heart. It was obvious to me that God was trying to speak to me about the hard heart I was trying in vain to hide. Something in the pit of my stomach stirred a little, but I tried to answer as innocently as possible, no, I hadn't spoken to him. I casually asked why she would ask such a question, hoping my smooth demeanour would satisfy Ruth's curiosity. It seemed to do the trick. I blithely reasoned that would be the end of it, but in my God-given conscience I knew that I had to let go of the hatred or else I would end up as bitter as Luke.

The following night I had a dream about Luke. I saw him as a little boy. He was drawing. I couldn't see what it was, but I was aware he was drawing out of a heart of love for God. In a strange way, it melted my heart at once. I was so impacted by this seemingly innocuous dream that I woke up crying.

Upon returning home, I felt compelled to reach out and speak to Luke. God did not want me to carry on holding the sin of unforgiveness in my heart. I had to make some sort of gesture towards him to free myself from my self-imposed prison. I struggled to think of some bland reason to get in touch with him, and remembered his daughter wanted me to lend him a book I had. He was surprised by my call and asked repeatedly what the real reason for contacting him was. The book ploy was evidently not enough to satisfy his curiosity. After repeated questioning, I confessed to the dream I had about him, which he thought was bizarre. I thought it was bizarre too, but in a different way. I was sure that it was God's prompting to get me to pick up the phone and give him a call. We spoke for an hour about various mundane things. Luke did not want to talk about the troubling experiences of our past, but I felt that this was a necessary step towards healing in our relationship. I learned a valuable lesson then about letting go of unforgiveness and of taking positive action against my negative attitudes and behaviours. Luke and I are not yet reconciled, but I am free from the curse of unforgiveness, which allows me to continue to pray for him according to God's will. However things turn out between us, I am free.

We must never allow the roots of unforgiveness to take hold in our hearts. By way of warning I have to say that unforgiveness will kill you. It will kill the sensitivity to the Holy Spirit in you, which in turn will kill the creativity and passion God has so carefully planted as a seed in your heart. Unforgiveness will destroy you if you allow its inky black poison into your soul. It will be like a bloodsucking leech that will mercilessly extract every simple joy and pleasure out of your God-given life. Where the path of life diverges, unforgiveness is the lower road; it will have you, it will take you down. The thrill of the fast descent into unforgiveness will soon be over when you hit the bottom of that dark pit of wilful self-indulgence. The further you go, the deader you become, until at last the devil applauds – not you, but himself. He can do no more, he only has loathing for you; not praise. You have chosen the road that leads down where he would have you, and all because of wilful pride.

The arrogance of an unforgiving spirit is deeply rooted in pride. Jesus tackled this form of arrogance in answer to a question from his disciple Peter:

> Then Peter came to him and asked, "Lord, how often should I forgive someone who sins against me? Seven times?" "No, not seven times," Jesus replied, "but seventy times seven! "Therefore, the Kingdom of Heaven can be compared to a king who decided to bring his accounts up to date with servants who had borrowed money from him. In the process, one of his debtors was brought in who owed him millions of dollars. He couldn't pay, so his master ordered that he be sold – along with his wife, his children, and everything he owned – to pay the debt.
>
> "But the man fell down before his master and begged him, 'Please, be patient with me, and I will pay it all.'

Then his master was filled with pity for him, and he released him and forgave his debt.

"But when the man left the king, he went to a fellow servant who owed him a few thousand dollars. He grabbed him by the throat and demanded instant payment.

"His fellow servant fell down before him and begged for a little more time. 'Be patient with me, and I will pay it,' he pleaded. But his creditor wouldn't wait. He had the man arrested and put in prison until the debt could be paid in full.

"When some of the other servants saw this, they were very upset. They went to the king and told him everything that had happened. Then the king called in the man he had forgiven and said, 'You evil servant! I forgave you that tremendous debt because you pleaded with me. Shouldn't you have mercy on your fellow servant, just as I had mercy on you?' Then the angry king sent the man to prison to be tortured until he had paid his entire debt.

"That's what my heavenly Father will do to you if you refuse to forgive your brothers and sisters from your heart."

Matthew 18:21–35 (NLT)

In God's sight, sin is sin. We, on the other hand, like to dress it up by whatever finery we can throw upon it, whether it is our own good works or measuring our sins against the sin of others. Our good works and futile comparisons with the bad deeds of others will always be plain old sin as far as God is concerned. Paul hits the nail on the head here:

> For everyone has sinned; we all fall short of
> God's glorious standard.

> Romans 3:23 (NLT)

This startling truth is what sticks in the craw of every self-righteous individual. "I've never killed anyone", "I am a good person at heart", "I have my share of flaws but I'm not a bad individual". No one ever measured up to God's righteous standard, except Jesus. We need to get our righteousness from him, not from our own good works, which God sees as good for nothing anyhow. The Old Testament prophet Isaiah lets no one off the hook either:

> We are all infected and impure with sin.
> When we display our righteous deeds, they
> are nothing but filthy rags.

> Isaiah 64:6 (NLT)

It requires humility to forgive others who have wronged us. Humility comes readily when we fix our gaze at the cross where Jesus, the perfect man who was God, died for the sins of the world. He did nothing wrong. He came to love us in his sinless perfection; our sin nailed him and held him fast to that wretched cross. Thankfully, the grave could not hold him. If we put our trust in Christ and follow his commands, we will enjoy life forever with him. It doesn't get any better than that.

The answer Jesus gave Peter that day was a fresh revelation concerning forgiveness. God has forgiven us a colossal debt. We deserved death for our sins, but he forgave our debts through the sacrifice of his only Son. Who are we to withhold forgiveness from others when Jesus forgave us our sins; the sins that meant his death? The apostle Paul adds perspective to Christ's forgiveness over us:

> But God shows his great love for us in this way: Christ died for us while we were still sinners.

> Romans 5:8

If you want to be a Christian – a real Christian, not a self-righteous religious person – you must make forgiveness a lifestyle choice. If Jesus did it, so can we. He knew we would cause him pain, he knew we would hurt others, tell lies, be proud and full of our own self-importance, but he chose to forgive us while we were still sinners. How can we do any less towards those who, like us, are made in the image of God?

Sometimes, forgiving seems a very difficult thing to do. There will be times when it appears impossible, but know this; by the grace of God it can be done. Determine in advance that forgiveness *will* be your lifestyle. Determine that Satan will not trick you down the lower road that leads to death and destruction. Refuse to be his tool. Do not let him trick you into thinking unforgiveness will achieve anything good in your life. As the saying goes, "Not forgiving someone is like drinking poison and expecting the other person to die." We are called to something better. As servants of God we are called to be loving ambassadors for Christ. If we live with the cross as our standard, however great the cost to ourselves, we will be transformed from the inside out. The end result will be that others will see the life-changing power of God working in us.

You may have never considered it this way, but forgiveness is a choice – it isn't about feelings. When you forgive someone, don't be surprised if old bitter memories or resentful feelings recur. The devil will endeavour to remind you of past wrongs made against you, but you must firmly resist his ploys to ensnare you. Determine to live in the victory of forgiveness. A great way to overcome when struggling to forgive someone is to pray God's blessings over the person who has wronged you. Pray that they will know and experience the same love that you have found in Christ. That will be a whopping black eye for hell.

Recently, Ruth and I have experienced painful betrayal at the hands of people who were once trusted friends. They sent emails and letters to our family, friends and several members our church. They wrote libellous accusations and lies about the leadership team and disclosed things about other members of our congregation that were of a sensitive and private nature, some of which were not even true, or if true, they were greatly distorted. We did our best to resolve the matter and tried in vain to meet with them privately by responding to their cruel behaviour with messages of love.

The saying goes that 'hurting people hurt people'. When we realise that the attacks against us are often misguided efforts of people trying to work out their pain, it can make it easier for us to forgive them.

It can be tempting to rehearse the faults and failures of others to your friends and family, but that is not going to help matters. In fact, it only spreads the pain. and possibly the resentment, further. Entrust your past hurts to God. Talking about them with whoever happens to have a listening ear will bring up feelings and resentments you would rather not have to deal with later on. It may be necessary to share past hurts where people have wronged us with a trusted friend who can listen and help us work through the pain and loss we have experienced at the hands of others.

The apostle Paul said God "has been very kind and patient, waiting for you to change, but you think nothing of his kindness. Perhaps you do not understand that God is kind to you so you will change your hearts and lives" (Romans 2:4). In the same way, God has been kind to you, so act in kindness towards others, even to those who hate you and say hurtful things about you. If we strive to be the humble people God calls us to be, we must be long-suffering with the weaknesses of others. Take some time out now to stop and reflect at how long-suffering God has been with you. Perhaps you were living a lukewarm life as a Christian, or you may have wilfully turned against the Father's heart. It might surprise you how much easier it will be to offer forgiveness to others once you have taken stock of the wealth of forgiveness God has given to you.

Forgiving does not mean excusing wilful, abusive behaviour, whether it is physical, emotional or spiritual. No one in God's Kingdom is expected to be a doormat. Do whatever it takes to get yourself to a safe place, away from a toxic relationship or dangerous situation.

Forgiving God may be something you need to tackle too. There are times in every Christian's life when they will feel let down or abandoned by God. Although he never abandons us, it may seem like he does when he is silent. It will be good to revisit those past feelings and hurts, especially with the help of a mentor or strong Christian friend who can help you to work through those issues.

Sometimes the Holy Spirit does such a good job of healing me from past hurts I can't believe those hurtful experiences actually happened to me. When I have shared my testimony of healing through forgiveness, it feels as if I am talking about someone else. If you make forgiveness a lifestyle, there will be so much settled peace in your heart you will be amazed. The prophet Isaiah said:

You will keep in perfect peace all who trust
in you, all whose thoughts are fixed on you!

Isaiah 26:3 (NLT)

Set your mind on God and his unrelenting forgiveness. Determine this will be your lifestyle choice and you will find him meeting you at every turn, helping you make it over seemingly impossible mountains of offence. There is so much rich living for us to do and enjoy than to waste it on the reeking rot of unforgiveness.

UNANSWERED PRAYER

We must go through many hardships to enter the
kingdom of God ...

Paul and Barnabas, Acts 14:22 (NIV)

Why does a child die, even when their parents have prayed fervently with faith for healing? Why does an unemployed man fail to find work, despite his steadfast prayers to secure work for months or even years? Or, consider a woman who musters the courage to face her sex abuser in court, only to find the jury unable to declare a guilty verdict. Why? This one word question has probably been asked billions of times the world over.

Answers to questions like these may be hard to uncover. In an age when it is so easy to find facts and figures on the Internet, we wish to find answers to life's probing questions in similar fashion, but we seek in vain. Giving us the answers to all of our questions isn't on God's agenda at all. He is far more interested in developing our character than our comfort in having every question answered.

Struggling with unanswered prayer can be a roadblock on the journey to being more like Jesus. We will experience times in our prayer lives when it feels like we are wading through sticky mud – the kind that sticks to the bottom of our feet until we feel like we are walking on platform shoes with lead soles. Every step takes great effort and even then we feel like we are sliding back, further away from our destination. Times like these call for a 'plodder', someone who will keep going regardless of how bleak the outlook.

Thirty years ago, my parents' marriage began to show some pretty severe cracks. Over the course of years, they had started to drift away from one another. The slipping away from love was unnoticeable at first, but towards the end of their faltering marriage it tore them apart like weak swimmers plunging helplessly over Niagara Falls. They separated acrimoniously in the year that was to be their twenty-fifth wedding anniversary. Because of the split, my immediate family fragmented and remains so to this day.

The whole situation had been drenched in the pain of loss over a failed marriage and broken relationships for over 28 years now. I cannot begin to tell of how frequently

I have prayed for the restoration of relationships between my parents and us children and between my siblings and me. At times it appeared as if my prayers had the opposite effect and strained relationships only became worse. The pain and breadth of this loss was vast. Over many years when I would sit and stare into space and repeatedly ask God, "Why?" I didn't see any redeeming value in the suffering of my family and others caught in the ugly wake of so many catastrophic divisions.

God has brought a lot of emotional healing to me, which has been fantastic. From time to time, the pain of the loss and my unanswered prayer rises to greet me in an unexpected tide of emotion. I discovered this over a year ago when Ruth and I had a holiday on the Atlantic coast of America to the very place where my family took our annual summer holidays. During the two weeks we spent there, I had plenty of time to reminisce over the great moments I shared with my grandparents, parents and siblings during those gloriously hot summers. The simple pleasures of those days were swimming and diving into the pounding waves of the Atlantic Ocean, fishing at Indian River Inlet – hoping to catch sea trout but catching lots of blues instead – crabbing, eating lots of pizza and walking along the boardwalk at Rehoboth Beach. The best part of those summers was meeting up with extended family and friends we hadn't seen since the last summer holiday. Altogether, these are the bittersweet memories of those halcyon days.

On the last day of our summer holiday last year, Ruth and I visited Lewes beach which held many of those wonderful childhood memories for me. As I waded into the blue-grey waters of Delaware Bay, all those emotion-filled memories flooded back in one single moment of pain and disappointment at all the unanswered prayers I had said for my family. I unexpectedly began to cry; my salty tears dropping pointlessly into the equally salty water surrounding me. I knew God had restored and healed so much in me that had been terribly broken, but the present sense of the deep losses I experienced were still there.

I discovered something more that day besides the recurring pain of my unanswered prayers and the searing emotional pain I had experienced. I learned it is hard to sob when swimming, but I managed. I suspect no one on the beach that day would have noticed the lone swimmer bobbing far out in Lewes Bay looking towards the lighthouse. There was one, however, who did, and he has been with me through it all, holding me along with my unanswered questions – my ever-present God.

Nicky Gumbel tweeted this about prayer which you may find helpful: "If God answers 'Yes', He is increasing your faith. If 'Wait', He is increasing your patience. If 'No', He has something better for you."[25] Although I can't understand God's answers or lack of answers to my prayers, I can and do know he is for me and not against me. This is very reassuring.

In times of unanswered prayer, we need the spiritual grit I spoke about earlier, for the Christian faith is simply this: faith. Faith requires that we don't know everything. We won't always have answers to life's hard questions, but we know God and he is enough. He will be there to guide us on through the pain of all our unanswered prayers. He will lovingly lead us to the quiet waters of his peace. He will, in fact, draw us to himself, for he is peace.

DISOBEDIENCE

Jesus of Nazareth always comes asking disciples to follow him – not merely "accept him," not merely "believe in him," not merely "worship him," but to follow him: one either follows Christ, or one does not. There is no compartmentalization of the faith, no realm, no sphere, no business, no politic in which the lordship of Christ will be excluded. We either make him Lord of all lords, or we deny him as Lord of any.

Lee Camp[26]

I guess I only fool myself
For I said I have yielded all
But in a secret corner of my heart
Was a kingdom that didn't fall
I surrender now, make my heart your throne
Rule it's kingdoms, great and small
For if you're not Lord of everything
Then you're not Lord at all

Author unknown

> Refusing to obey the Lord is as sinful as
> using evil magic. Being proud is as evil as
> worshiping statues of gods.

1 Samuel 15:23 (NIRV)

In my time of discipling people, I have seen numerous instances where people are progressing nicely on their journey of faith. They are zealous in their Bible reading, prayer life, attendance at church, and are passionate in sharing their faith with non-believers, but something happens which draws them to a screeching halt like a speeding driver chancing upon a child in the road ahead of them. Their roadblock is disobedience. It might be the Holy Spirit has convicted them about some sin in the past that needs to be dealt with; perhaps there are apologies to be made, or there is a relationship that is getting too sexual and boundaries are being crossed. Whatever it may be, what happens next is the pivot on which the whole of their spiritual life turns – obedience. The decision to follow Jesus is in the balance.

Left unchecked, disobedience will inevitably lead people to a place of deep spiritual poverty which they will usually deny even exists. Disobedient people have a tendency to throw up smokescreens as to why they have chosen to go against God's commands. Excuses abound: "The Church is full of hypocrites", "I don't need to go to church, I need to spend more time with my family", "The Bible doesn't really mean that when it says …"

Some backsliding Christians wilfully head into adulterous relationships when they start justifying their sinful behaviour with things like, "I'm connecting with this person on a spiritual level." They foolishly ignore the fact the writer of Hebrews warned:

> All of you should honor marriage. You should keep the marriage bed pure. God will judge the person who commits adultery. He will judge everyone who commits sexual sins.
>
> Hebrews 13:4 (NIRV)

That is plain enough. God warns against these behaviours because he knows when we go against what is pure, we only ask for trouble and pain. He doesn't want that for his sons and daughters he loves so much.

One bizarre excuse a young person gave me for his choice in living a promiscuous lifestyle was the Church of England became an institution in order that Henry VIII could divorce his wife. He wrongly reasoned we shouldn't trust any teaching that comes out of the Church. If anyone wants an excuse to sin, they will find one.

Rarely will a person admit they have decided to go their own way. Only a couple of times has anyone ever said to me that they want to discard their faith because they simply want to sin. Sin is very deceitful; if left unchecked it will have its victim in isolation to anyone who would attempt to help. Dietrich Bonhoeffer's words have no less truth than they did over seventy years ago: "Sin demands to have a man by himself. It withdraws him from the community. The more isolated a person is, the more destructive will be the power of sin over him."[27]

Cain was one such man who foolishly set up his own roadblock of disobedience.

> When they grew up, Abel became a shepherd, while Cain cultivated the ground. When it was time for the harvest, Cain presented some of his crops as a gift to the LORD. Abel also brought a gift – the best of the firstborn lambs from his flock. The LORD accepted Abel and his gift, but he did not accept Cain and his gift. This made Cain very angry, and he looked dejected.

> "Why are you so angry?" the LORD asked Cain. "Why do you look so dejected? You will be accepted if you do what is right. But if you refuse to do what is right, then watch out! Sin is crouching at the door, eager to control you. But you must subdue it and be its master."

> Genesis 4:2–7 (NLT)

God, the maker of heaven and earth, is giving Cain a helpful lesson on obedience and the danger of sin. No one could have warned him better, yet what does he do? He goes it alone and does his own thing, which ultimately leads to him murdering his brother out of jealousy. One of the saddest things about Cain's life is that when he was growing up with Abel, he would never have imagined killing his brother. This is the danger of sin; it will take a person further than they would ever have imagined. Later on, in Genesis 4:13, when having to deal with the consequences of his sin, Cain says to the Lord, "My punishment is too great for me to bear!" (NLT)

Sin was sneakily crouching at Cain's door, but he was too foolish to give it any regard, and as a result he suffered a harsh penalty for giving in to it. We can learn a lesson from Cain's downfall. There is a major problem with managing sin; it cannot be managed by anyone. In fact, sin will manage a person more than they could ever imagine if they yield to its immeasurable temptations. This is why the writer of Hebrews warns against the treachery of sin:

> But encourage one another daily, as long as
> it is called 'Today', so that none of you may
> be hardened by sin's deceitfulness.
>
> Hebrews 3:13 (NIVUK)

When she was nineteen, a woman called Alicia was introduced to regeneration Church by a friend from her sixth form. She shares her story here about how God challenged her to deal with her issues of disobedience:

If I am honest, I only went along to an outreach event to keep him quiet. The speaker, Ruth Poch, was one of the pastors at regeneration – what she said impressed me. I visited every now and then but decided to go to an Alpha course held in the spring of 2005. Both occasions led me to attend Hillsong Church (with the same friend who invited me to regeneration) and make a commitment to follow Christ. I had experienced a break-up from a fairly toxic relationship and was asking serious questions about life at this time, but I would still say that it was a fairly impulsive decision. I knew that I was searching for meaning, but at the moment I raised my hand in response to the appeal, I had not considered the cost or implications of following Jesus.

Ruth and I began a mentoring relationship soon after. Although it was informal, she met with me regularly and intentionally. After about ten months of attending regeneration, it was time for me to go to university. This was a real decision-making point for me. Was I prepared to be identified with Jesus, with all that might cost me? The answer, in reality, was no. I signed up to various clubs and took part in their initiations. Hockey quickly became very important and going to church and prioritising my faith soon became a distant memory. As I settled into university culture – a heavy drinking, partying lifestyle – Ruth kept making the effort to stay in touch and maintain the relationship. If I am honest, she was acting as a mirror that I didn't want to look into. I understood enough truth to be uncomfortable with the life I was leading, but not enough to be willing to give any of it up.

Things came to a head in a very difficult telephone conversation with Ruth when I essentially told her that she was wasting her time with me and should leave me alone. I said some harsh things because I didn't know how else to get her to understand that I wanted to be left alone. I remember quite clearly from the conversation crying myself to sleep. On reflection, I was working from the misunderstanding that, in order to be part of the church, I needed to 'have it all together'. After ending the mentoring relationship and distancing myself from the regen community I continued in my compromised lifestyle until I graduated from university in 2010. For the entire three years of university life, I felt conflict – neither completely joining in with the most broken aspects of the student lifestyle, nor doing more than attending church casually during the holidays. I couldn't find satisfaction in either place.

After graduation, I came back to regen as it had never really lost its appeal to me. What really changed my direction was eventually being offered the opportunity to join the leadership team and assume more responsibility. It was explained to me very clearly what was involved – a serious commitment to Jesus and His church. From the first days of fragile faith, I had been drawn to the church and impacted by the Bible. I now had a clear opportunity to count the cost of following Jesus and chose to accept it. Ruth had never wavered in her commitment to me. Now our relationship had a new foundation and could develop. It hasn't been an easy road, but once I chose obedience, I never regretted the journey.

Alicia knew God was requiring her to be obedient to his Word, but there were sins in her life she was not willing to give up. Like Cain, she knew what God was requiring of her, but she did not have the desire to circumvent the roadblock of disobedience in order to live her life God's way. It wasn't until Alicia let go and made the decision to choose obedience that she found contentment and peace on her journey. She has flourished as a leader in our church and has encouraged so many others in her life of faith. None of this would have been possible if she had not chosen to travel the long road of obedience.

An anonymous person once said, "Sin will take you farther than you want to go, keep you longer than you want to stay, and cost you more than you want to pay." When left unchecked, sin will cost us our souls, which it is why it is essential to have someone who can speak into our lives and warn us of the deceitfulness of sin, like Ruth did with Alicia. Don't behave like Cain; instead, determine that you will do whatever God is asking you to. Don't reject his commands and turn them into roadblocks; instead, let them become stepping stones to take you higher on your journey to the Promised Land of acceptance and reward.

Godly obedience is the only way to life. This simple proverb points us in the right direction: "Anyone who loves learning accepts correction, but a person who hates being corrected is stupid" (Proverbs 12:1). If you think about it, when have you ever regretted obedience? Enough said.

LACK OF SELF-CONFIDENCE

Though an army besiege me,
my heart will not fear;
though war break out against me,
even then I will be confident.

Psalm 27:3 (NIV)

When I was young, I had little confidence in my abilities or myself. I wasn't sporty, and was only an average student without any obvious natural talent. I didn't excel in anything in particular, and when I did make an effort to succeed, it felt like all I did was fail. Most of the time I felt like a loser, and that was the image I sometimes projected. It has taken me years to overcome those feelings of insecurity and self-doubt that plagued me in my youth. A lack of self-confidence is a real joy stealer and, more than that, it is unbiblical. Every Christian should have self-confidence. Perhaps a more correct word for self-confidence in this instance should be 'God-confidence'.

When we get to grips with the fact that God loves us with an everlasting love that is unrelenting and that he is always for us, no matter how we feel about ourselves, we should be confident. When we are confident in God, we can do great exploits for him. Satan knows this and will do whatever he can to have a go at undermining any confidence we may have.

One of our young leaders is a great guy called Matt. God has helped him tremendously concerning his lack of self-confidence. Here is his story:

> Leadership is never something I saw in my life when I was younger. I never expected or even wanted to grow into a leader; in fact, I grew up in a church serving in the background, allowing others to step up and lead. That was my church experience for the first sixteen years of my life.
>
> When I joined regeneration, I continued to serve in the background, expecting to remain in the shadows while others led. However, James and Ruth noticed something in me that I had not yet seen in myself: the gift of leadership. They chose to take a risk and start developing that gift within me, but looking back I know it wasn't an easy process! I had previously lived my life terrified of the extra responsibility and attention that came with leading, and for me this lack of confidence was a huge hurdle to overcome. And yet James, Ruth and other members of the leadership team at regeneration faithfully supported and encouraged me and taught me about what true leadership meant, while giving me opportunities to practise this newly discovered gift within the church. As a result, I was invited onto the leadership team of the church when I was seventeen and given the role of leading a guys' discipleship group. This was monumental in my development, as I was given the

opportunity to surround myself with some really inspirational leaders and grow from their example.

I began to accept the role I was given and lead the discipleship group, although even then I still battled self-confidence issues and timidity. I was always the quietest at a leadership meeting! But, in time, and with James and Ruth constantly encouraging me to speak out more and grow my confidence, I saw a transformation in me that shifted from fearful and doubtful to confident and courageous. Since that point, I've had the privilege of leading young leader projects, youth events and clubs, and youth-focused discipleship groups.

When I reflect and think about the person I am today, I know it is only through God's grace and the transforming power of his Holy Spirit that I can lead, and yet I am so thankful that James and Ruth saw something in a shy, introverted sixteen-year-old boy and chose to take a risk in raising him into a leader. I know I still have so much to learn about leadership, and there are plenty of times I still get it wrong, but ultimately I know I'm surrounded by a community of people that love me and are willing to continue investing in me.

This encouraging testimony from Matt reminds me that this is what it's all about. Discipling others is such a privilege. I love seeing how people grow when they accept the challenge to move out from their comfort zones. We are so grateful that Matt took the risk of trying something new. He came to discover that when a person submits to the lordship of Jesus Christ, they can accomplish things they would never imagine.

Let's take a look at three men in the Bible who had to deal with their low levels of self-confidence.

Moses, Gideon and Saul achieved breath-taking victories many of their contemporaries would have loved to realise. Their stories are the meaty stuff of Sunday school lessons, but perhaps we don't take appropriate time to peer back to the very humble beginnings of these famous men of valour as they struggled with their personal demons of self-doubt.

It seems reasonable to surmise that if God were to suddenly appear and ask you to do some great exploit, there wouldn't be any point in arguing with him. Who wants to argue with God? Moses was foolishly ready for this challenge. The following is what he (shockingly) had to say to God's request that he go be a deliverer for a nation of two and a half to three million people:

> Then Moses answered, "What if the people of Israel do not believe me or listen to me? What if they say, 'The LORD did not appear to you'?"

Exodus 4:1

> But Moses said to the LORD, "Please, Lord, I have never been a skilled speaker. Even now, after talking to you, I cannot speak well. I speak slowly and can't find the best words."

Exodus 4:10

But Moses said, "Please, Lord, send someone else."

Exodus 4:13

Moses' attitude hardly makes him a strong candidate for a liberator of a nation destined to become greater than their wildest dreams. The saying, "God's will is God's bill" is as true for you and me as it was for Moses. It wasn't easy for him, but as Moses obediently answered the call of God, he was able not only to deliver the Children of Israel from the mighty nation of Egypt, but to lead them faithfully and skilfully for forty years throughout their wilderness wanderings. Yes, he made mistakes along the way. Who doesn't? But he was faithful to the call and found God to be very strong on his behalf. Legend.

Flipping forward nearly three hundred years later, we find the Children of Israel are having quite a difficult time. They foolishly did what the Lord said was wrong. So for seven torturous years, the Lord handed them over to their enemies from Midian. The Midianites were very powerful and cruel to Israel. The Israelites had to make hiding places in the mountains and caves and any other safe places they could find. Whenever the Israelites planted crops, the Midianites and other people would come and attack them. They destroyed the crops that the Israelites had planted and left nothing for Israel to eat and, as a result, Israel became very poor. Finally, in their desperation, they cried out to the Lord.

The Lord had brought them out of the land of slavery with his strong arm by the hand of Moses where he told them, "I am the LORD your God. Live in the land of the Amorites, but do not worship their gods" (Judges 6:10). But they didn't obey him; hence the Midianites appear at the command of God. Nothing brings clarity to a situation quite like a healthy dose of persecution.

Now, let's draw the curtain back on the next act of this unfolding drama:

> The angel of the LORD appeared to Gideon and said, "The LORD is with you, mighty warrior!" Then Gideon said, "Sir, if the LORD is with us, why are we having so much trouble? Where are the miracles our ancestors told us he did when the LORD brought them out of Egypt? But now he has left us and has handed us over to the Midianites."

> The LORD turned to Gideon and said, "Go with your strength and save Israel from the Midianites. I am the one who is sending you." But Gideon answered, "Lord, how can I save Israel? My family group is the weakest in Manasseh, and I am the least important member of my family."

> Judges 6:12–15

Here we go again with another young man questioning the direct call of God. Moses may have had some excuse for his hesitation, but Gideon had none. Moses' example was too hard for him to learn from and take to heart. Nevertheless, God will have his man, or woman. Gideon led Israel into victory as Moses had also done before him. First, he needed to put out a fleece, literally, before he would venture any further. He eventually yielded to God's call and the rest, as they say, is history.

If you were looking for a man who was head and shoulders above the rest, that would be Saul. He was the original 'head and shoulders above the rest' kind of guy. This Old Testament story is where we most likely get this saying from. Saul was called to lead Israel as their first king and, without question, this would have been a daunting task. Saul didn't have the confidence that he could wear the crown and carry all of the responsibilities that went along with it.

When the time came for the prophet Samuel to choose by lot a king for Israel, he called all the tribes of Israel to stand before him. As Samuel moved among them, I'm sure there were quite a few young men who were jostling one another to be at the foremost position. None of them were chosen. Saul was God's elect, but where was he? Hiding among the luggage. Hardly a suitable candidate for the first king of Israel, or so you would think. Saul was God's man for the hour, but he obviously didn't have enough confidence in himself to even slink to the back of his clan. He went further than that; he hid among the baggage.

Saul went on to become a great king for Israel and performed many great exploits for God before he allowed pride to get the better of him.

These three men had one thing in common besides their glaring lack of self-confidence; they allowed God to use them despite their lack. The Lord's awesome power was displayed in those timid guys. Isn't that great news for us too? God delights to use people who don't necessarily think of themselves as capable to undertake exploits for the Kingdom. This way, whatever we do, all glory will go to God.

Do you think God can't or won't use you? Don't be like those three who initially balked at God's call. The Lord has a job for every one of us to do and it doesn't matter if we think we can't do it. Like the apostle Paul, we can each declare, "I can do all things through Christ who strengthens me" (Philippians 4:13, NKJV).

BLIND SPOTS

… memories are the key not to the past, but to the future. I know that the experiences of our lives, when we let God use them, become the mysterious and perfect preparation for the work He will give us to do.

Corrie ten Boom[28]

When you hold on to your history, you do it at the expense of your destiny.

Bishop T.D. Jakes[29]

The longer you can look back, the farther you can look forward.

Winston Churchill[30]

Driving a car can be an exciting experience, especially when travelling out on the open road with no traffic jams; only quiet roads with fantastic panoramic views. I love driving if I am on a road trip to somewhere I have never been before. As exciting as road trips are, there are hazards every driver needs to be aware of if they want to arrive safely at their destination.

When I moved to England, I had to take a driving test, despite having an American driving licence. Everything seemed to go well with my road test until the examiner quizzed me about pulling out into the flow of traffic.

"What things do you need to do before pulling into a lane, Mr Poch?"

"Take off the emergency brake."

"Yes, and after that?"

"Check my mirrors."

"Yes, and after that?"

By the stern look on his face (he wasn't directly looking at me, probably because he had disdain for people like me who should know better) and by the tone of his voice, I had the distinct feeling that I wasn't going to walk away with a 100 per cent score on my test. "Signal". This time my answer sounded more like a question due to my weakening confidence.

"Yes, and after that?"

"Pull carefully into traffic?"

"No, you are missing something out, Mr Poch!"

"Er, uh, look over my shoulder before pulling out?" I offered weakly.

"Yes! Why don't you try doing it sometime?"

I inexplicably walked away with a pass that day, along with an essential admonition to check for blind spots when pulling out into the road.

A blind spot in a vehicle is an area around it that cannot be directly observed by the driver. There are other kinds of transport that have no blind spots at all, such as bicycles, motorcycles and horses. Pedestrians don't have blind spots either, but one thing is certain – on our journeys through life we all have 'blind spots' which can create problems for us if we don't look over our shoulder occasionally.

There will be periods in our discipleship where we will need to look back into our past in order to understand how we managed to get where we are. This may be tremendously uncomfortable, but it will be helpful if we are to move forward into the life Jesus has for us.

Naomi came to our church a year ago and discovered the importance of looking back in order to move forward:

> I was born into a Christian household and a happy church life. When I was younger, church was the

highlight of my week and was where I met my very best friends. However, at around the age of six, the happy family life and happy church life I knew fell apart. My parents divorced and the church I was in dismantled due to an affair. My mum was left to raise me and my brothers alone and we proceeded to try and go to another church and rebuild our trust in church and leadership again. After many years of not really finding our 'fit' as a family, I eventually found a church when I was around fifteen that seemed right. I poured my life into this church, but once again found myself being betrayed by the people in leadership there. This essentially led me to have a huge distrust in Church and those who lead it.

My faith became somewhat of a 'me and God' kind of faith. I convinced myself that this was the only way to do it and the best way to do it. I loved God, but I wasn't willing to trust his Church. This didn't stop me from going; I still went, largely week in week out, but I would never go too deep or allow people to really speak into my life.

When I returned from university, I joined regeneration and it was here that God began to really challenge me. I had felt that it was right to be in the mentoring programme that the church ran and allow someone to speak into my life. It was in this setting that I began to unpack what had gone on in my past and deal with the former hurts from my church life. After a lot of conversation and much prayer, I began to see things more clearly and came to understand that I was being robbed of so much by allowing my past hurts to dictate my future. I had allowed those hurts to harden my heart towards receiving from others, particularly those at church.

I began to name and forgive those people that had hurt me and release myself from the burden of carrying all of that pain. In doing this, I began to see how much I had believed the lie that it was OK for it to be 'me and God'. I realised that although my personal and intimate relationship with God is what is of utmost importance, it should never be at the expense of allowing community and Church to also speak into your life. It was when the two were working together that I began to see breakthrough in so many areas of my life and I felt the weight of those issues fall away.

Many Christians today can find themselves stuck spiritually like Naomi was, simply because they will not deal with their past hurts or failures. They are unable to move forward in their spiritual lives because they will not go back and address the hurts, disappointments and mistakes they made in the past. These issues are like blind spots, which, if left unchecked, will cause problems for the journey ahead. It takes courage and strength to deal with the past, but with God's help we can experience tremendous restoration and healing when we deal with our 'blind spots'.

CONDEMNATION AND SHAME

Shame, shame, I know your name.

Anon

When you are guilty, it is not your sins you hate but yourself.[31]

Anthony de Mello

The final roadblocks I want to look at are the evil doppel-gangers of condemnation and shame. These heinous devils sit on the shoulders of many Christians and whisper insidious lies in their ears that what they have done is beyond the pale and is unforgiveable and disgusting. The real stink of all of this is that these devils drive the same people to commit sin in the first place. Little wonder that the devil gets a mention for this behaviour in the book of Revelation:

> For the accuser of our brothers and sisters, who accuses them before our God day and night, has been hurled down.

Revelation 12:10 (NIVUK)

It is good to have a heads-up on this one, since condemna-tion and shame are two of the devil's favourite roadblocks to demoralise and decommission Christians. The great news is that we don't have to entertain condemnation and shame for one second. God holds out his grace towards us in the most amazing way. We don't have to work hard in our own efforts to please God. Brennan Manning strikes a blow against this erroneous way of thinking in his very direct way:

Our huffing and puffing to impress God, our scram-bling for brownie points, our thrashing about trying to fix ourselves while hiding our pettiness and wallowing in guilt are nauseating to God and are a flat out denial of the gospel of grace.[32]

This gospel of grace that Brennan is talking about is the gospel we believe in, but at times don't really live out. It is one thing to know about grace in our heads, but it is another to know it in our hearts. Have a look at what the apostle John had to say to people who were struggling with guilt:

> This is the way we know that we belong to the way of truth. When our hearts make us feel guilty, we can still have peace before God. God is greater than our hearts, and he knows everything. My dear friends, if our hearts do not make us feel guilty, we can come without fear into God's presence. And God gives us what we ask for because we obey God's commands and do what pleases him.
>
> 1 John 3:19–22

A young woman I know found spiritual healing for her soul in a remarkable way. She discovered that condemnation and guilt have no power of control in the heart of a Christian. Here is her story:

> The thief comes to kill, steal and destroy all that God has for us. I have experienced this first hand and can say that without the discipleship, mentorship, and deliverance ministries the Lord has sovereignly led me to I would still be shackled by heavy burdens and oppression.

A couple of years back I was in a very dark and overwhelming place; mentally, emotionally and spiritually. My view and perception of the Christian walk was a heavy religious burden I couldn't carry. A religious mentality had its grip on me and was keeping me from enjoying life and enjoying the Lord. My walk was one focused on behavior modification and religious dos and don'ts. This always led to pride, debilitating condemnation and zero joy in me.

The Lord intervened; he delivered me and deposited a hope and a joy in me that I had not known before. Through times of prayer, fellowship, confession and deliverance with the ministry at regeneration, I was set free. The Lord deposited a new hope in me. A severely heavy weight was lifted off my shoulders.

I also experienced a Christian lifestyle I had never seen before. It was eye opening, it was encouraging, it was refreshing, it was relieving more than anything else to see Christians of all ages fully given to the Lord. Interestingly to me they had something going on that surprised me. They possessed a freedom, a joy, a child-like faith that was incredibly attractive. I noticed that although life wasn't perfect or easy, they enjoyed the Lord. They spoke of their walk with a God they knew and even enjoyed! Like having a fun best friend you love to talk with and spend time and explore with! Full surrender, joy and freedom in Jesus was a combination I wanted.

I had been stressing out, the pastoral care I received comforted me by reminding me that God knew my heart, he had a plan, I need not worry. Pastor James told me, just relax; have fun, enjoy yourself, enjoy your days; Trust God. Just trust him with childlike faith. It was a simple message, but one I had not experienced firsthand.

I've learned how critically important discipleship is. The enemy will try to constantly deceive; it can become easy to forget the simplicity of the gospel. But it has been in times of discipleship and time with other believers that I'm redirected back to the truth that is freedom and joy in Jesus.

No wonder the original Greek for the word 'gospel' means 'good news'. God is greater than our hearts. Beyond what our hearts tell us, we need to listen to what God is telling us through the truth of his Word. There are many passages of Scripture that remind us of what God has done for us in regard to our sins. Take this one for instance:

> He has taken our sins away from us as far as
> the east is from west.

Psalm 103:12

King David knew that he had a lot to be forgiven for and he understood that when God accomplishes something, he doesn't do a half-baked job. David took hold of the truth of God's great forgiveness and this was before Christ, when the punishment for sin was the sacrifice of an animal.

Of course, we don't just keep on sinning because of the awesome grace of God. Some people erroneously think we can.

The actress Keira Knightley purportedly said she was desperate to be a Catholic because she would just be able to ask for forgiveness, which sounded much better that having to live with guilt; and that if she wasn't an atheist she could get away with anything, just ask for forgiveness and be forgiven.[33]

Keira understands the premise of grace in part, but not fully. We can ask God for forgiveness and find that forgiveness through the shed blood of Jesus, but we don't ask with the intention of continuing to sin. We ask God to forgive us so that we can move from sin to the life of holiness that God has called us to live in Jesus Christ. Would a child truly love their parents if they continually disobeyed, knowing they could rock up anytime and ask forgiveness? On the flip side, would a parent truly love their child if they just kept forgiving them for their disobedience, but didn't do anything to instruct them in how to live an obedient life and hold them to account? This is where conviction of sin comes in, which is miles better than condemnation or shame. The Holy Spirit convicts us for the wrong things we have done, but he never puts shame upon us; only the devil deals in shame. Jesus has come to give us life. The life of Jesus naturally deposits effervescent joy and peace into our hearts. This is the life we are called to experience as followers of Jesus. This really is 'good news'.

SEVEN

THAT OLD SIN PROBLEM

Let us think about each other and help each other to show love and do good deeds. You should not stay away from the church meetings, as some are doing, but you should meet together and encourage each other. Do this even more as you see the day coming.

Hebrews 10:24–25

What each one honours before all else, what before all things he admires and loves, this for him is God.

Origen

In keeping silent about evil, in burying it so deep within us that no sign of it appears on the surface, we are implanting it, and it will rise up a thousand fold in the future.

Aleksandr Solzhenitsyn[34]

I have swept away your sins like a cloud. I have scattered your offenses like the morning mist.

Oh, return to me, for I have paid the price to set you free.

Isaiah 44:22 (NLT)

How can we help people who are struggling with an area of sin, which refuses to budge no matter how much leverage is brought to bear upon it? The enemy uses numerous tactics to snare people into sin. One of his greatest weapons to keep people in bondage is secrecy.

Back when I was sixteen, I struggled with strong feelings of lust – as any boy at that age most likely would. I couldn't control them and I felt very guilty about it. Plan A: I prayed and asked Jesus to forgive me and asked him to take the lust away. Nothing changed. Since Plan A wasn't working, I decided to go with Plan B, which was to tell someone about it. I struggled to think of who I could disclose my innermost secrets to. I knew if I could talk with someone and get them to pray for me, I would be able to get a handle on the torrents of lustful thoughts plaguing my mind. I felt too embarrassed to tell my dad about it. My younger brother wasn't an option, and as for my church, there wasn't a culture of accountability which would allow for a young person like me to offload and share my struggles and temptations with sin.

This practice of being open about sin problems was largely unheard of in the churches of the United States then. My desperate and crazy solution was to write a letter to a television evangelist, telling him of my lust dilemma and asking him to pray for me. I remember the frightening walk to the mailbox. My heart was pounding. Would someone see what I was doing and rip the letter out of my hand and read it aloud for the entire neighbourhood to hear? In the US, if we want to mail a letter, we put it in a tin mailbox at the end of the driveway and flip up a red metal flag, indicating to the mailman there is a letter waiting to be collected. When the letter was finally collected and that crimson flag went down, I breathed a sigh of relief. Momentarily I felt better, but soon after I began to worry. What if the television evangelist read my letter out on television? What if he wrote to my parents telling them what a miserable sinner I was? I needn't have worried. I never had an answer from him, but I did get begging letters from his organisation asking me to send money. So much for Plan B.

The memory of that incident gave me a purpose of wanting to ensure no one has to go through the torment of secrecy I suffered at sixteen. I was paranoid. I wish it had been different then for people like me who didn't have anyone to share their struggles over sin with.

Every church needs a culture of openness and vulnerability, where people are free to be open about their struggles with sin without fear of ridicule or shame. Here's what the apostle John had to say about it:

> This is the message we have heard from him
> and proclaim to you, that God is light, and

in him is no darkness at all. If we say we have fellowship with him while we walk in darkness, we lie and do not practice the truth. But if we walk in the light, as he is in the light, we have fellowship with one another, and the blood of Jesus his Son cleanses us from all sin.

1 John 1:5–7 (ESV)

To be able to walk in the light by means of accountability is a wonderful blessing every Christian should be able to experience. The devil hates it when Christians are accountable to one another in love because he knows when people share their struggles with sin it loses its controlling grip on them.

Sam is a young man in our church has had his fair share of temptations, and by his own admission, a number of failures. Despite this, he has soldiered on as a radical confessor and has made wonderful progress on his journey of discipleship:

I have struggled with lust for many years, and it rears its ugly head in various ways at different times. Sometimes it has been within a relationship where pushing healthy and godly boundaries seems more appealing than honouring the other person and God. Other times, it is the ongoing struggle against pornography, or it is the wandering eyes while out and about. Lust is a big issue in today's society because we are surrounded by provocative images and so it is a constant battle for many.

Repeatedly I have fallen short in this area. It can be scary telling someone where you are struggling and when you have messed up. Often, in my humanity, I try to keep things to myself: "What if this person judges me or tells my secret to the church?" or "I can't confess again, I will be letting that person down so I will keep it to myself." The enemy wraps us up in lies like this, but it is important to push through.

Sharing my struggles with lust has meant that the journey towards healing and wholeness has begun. Each time I struggle and each time I fall, I confess to God and tell my accountability partner (or mentor). Knowing that other people are there to support you, pray for you and spur you on is such a blessing. I have come to discover that the Christian life is not meant to be done alone, but in community. There is real strength in sharing our burdens and praying together.

I still struggle, but I struggle a lot less than I did before. I have decided to be a radical confessor – that's the way to grow: to confess quickly even when I really don't want to or feel like I need to. When we confess, the enemy loses his grip on us. Secrecy is the only weapon he has, but by walking in the light, we can be free from the fear and power that sin has over us.

Thankfully, Sam discovered that one of the devil's favourite tactics to defeat Christians is to divide and conquer. If he can get us to think we can make the journey of discipleship on our own, in isolation from a worshipping community, he is winning. When we isolate ourselves from other believers, we are more prone to his deceptive lies that our struggles against sin are hopeless. His full intention is that we give in to his lies, hide our assailing sins and bear the weight of guilt and shame he loves to burden us with. In answer to this tactic, every Christian needs to walk in the opposite direction – straight through the open doors of the church.

Jesus' brother, James, encouraged early Christians to live transparent lives like this:

> Confess your sins to each other and pray for each other so God can heal you. When a believing person prays, great things happen.

James 5:16

The apostle Paul encouraged the Colossian Christians to be honest with one another and put away their old practices:

> Do not lie to each other, since you have taken off your old self with its practices and have put on the new self, which is being renewed in knowledge in the image of its Creator.

Colossians 3:9–10 (NIVUK)

Confessing our sins to one another is a biblical mandate. We cannot enjoy the fullest level of Kingdom freedom if we fail to obey this power-inducing command. James links confession and prayer together. These two ingredients are essential for healing and growth in any accountability partnership.

At regen, we also suggest that people might want to ask two or three people they trust to honestly and lovingly tell them three things they need to improve on. It may sound a bit cringe worthy, but there is no better way to experience rapid growth in your spiritual development than to take part in this practice, not once, but regularly.

There is nothing like the Church. Where else can you go to find such loving and honest support to be the best person you can possibly be?

EIGHT

THE SELF-DECEPTION
OF HAPPY SINNERS

I am happy not believing, and that's what the evangelists don't seem to understand.

John Diamond[35]

Good friends, good books and a sleepy conscience: this is the ideal life.

Mark Twain[36]

Don't be misled – you cannot mock the justice of God. You will always harvest what you plant.

Galatians 6:7 (NLT)

I USED TO BELIEVE THAT all unrepentant people were unhappy. In my early upbringing in the Church, I was taught that people who are living a life of sin are miserable, but in my experience, I have observed people who are living sinful lifestyles whooping it up on the town, seemingly without a worry or care. Some Christians might think they are probably crying on their pillow most nights when no one is watching. That may well be true, but the Bible specifically mentions people who are quite happy living lives of unbridled sin:

> By faith Moses, when he was come to years, refused to be called the son of Pharaoh's daughter; choosing rather to suffer affliction with the people of God, than to enjoy the pleasures of sin for a season ...
>
> Hebrews 11:24–25 (KJV)

> For I envied the arrogant when I saw the prosperity of the wicked.
>
> They have no struggles; their bodies are healthy and strong. They are free from common human burdens; they are not plagued by human ills.
>
> Psalm 73:3–5 (NIVUK)

The Bible is clear: living a life of sin for some people can be pleasurable. Sinners may be happy, healthy people who seemingly have no problems, but what we must fully be aware of is that such happiness derived from sinful pleasures will not last. The writer of Hebrews acknowledges the "pleasures of sin", but he also clarifies the statement with three words, "for a season". That's the rub for sinners. Gratification from immoral behaviour will not last because every action will have a reaction. Paul clearly warned the Galatians about this:

> Those who live only to satisfy their own sinful nature will harvest decay and death from that sinful nature.

> Galatians 6:8 (NLT)

It is tragic and dangerous to treat the holy demands of God with contempt. Don't think for a minute that anyone will ultimately get away with living an immoral, self-centred lifestyle. Actions have consequences, and the greatest consequence of sin is that it separates us from a loving and gracious God.

When Jesus was entering Jerusalem towards the end of his ministry on earth, he spoke these words of both longing and rebuke over that rebellious city:

> O Jerusalem, Jerusalem, the city that kills the prophets and stones God's messengers! How often I have wanted to gather your children together as a hen protects her chicks beneath her wings, but you wouldn't let me. And now, look, your house is abandoned and desolate.

> Matthew 23:37–38 (NLT)

Many people in Jerusalem were clearly happy with not accepting the Messiah. How tragic. Jesus' desire for us is so strong. He desires that we would know the delight of obedience to him which goes far beyond the shallow happiness gained from sinful pleasures. Don't let the sometimes happy way of sin rob you of the insuppressible joy of eternal life with God.

NINE

JUST POINT ME IN THE RIGHT DIRECTION

God has made us what we are. In Christ Jesus, God
made us to do good works, which God planned in
advance for us to live our lives doing.

Ephesians 2:10

Efforts and courage are not enough without purpose
and direction.

John F. Kennedy[37]

All the days planned for me were written in your
book before I was one day old.

Psalm 139:16

S AMUEL JOHNSON WISELY SAID, "People need to be
reminded more often than they need to be instructed."
Which brings me to the point I cannot emphasise enough:
discipling people is *not* about telling them what to do. People
who change and become more like Jesus will do so when they
desire to, not when someone forces or coerces them to change.

It can be hard to watch people make bad choices after we have pointed them in the right direction, but the message of the cross involves choice and the free will of the followers of Jesus. It is imperative for any discipler to appreciate they will never be able to change anyone in the long-term. The people we love and watch over may do things to please us, but if their actions are not tied to their heart's desire for God, they will not be able to sustain any change. Only the Holy Spirit can bring about lasting change in the heart of a believer.

So, how do we help a disciple to follow Jesus above everything else? In Psalm 73, we find an old marker which points us in the right direction. The psalmist's heart has become bitter against God and he nearly loses his faith when he observes wicked and proud people prospering while he himself is trying his best to live a holy life in spite of his suffering. Life appears unfair, but then he goes to the Lord's temple and it is there that he gains perspective and his attitude changes. He says:

> I have no one in heaven but you;
> I want nothing on earth besides you.
> My body and my mind may become weak,
> but God is my strength.
> He is mine forever.
>
> Psalm 73:25–26

It is in the Lord's holy temple where he gets his revelation. What is happening there in the temple? People are bringing their sacrifices in worship to God; there is singing, prayer and reading of Scripture. The people of God are gathered in praise and worship. Nothing will give us perspective on what matters in life like seeing the Church in action in this way.

When I walk down the high street in Romford, I look into the faces of the people going by and I see a lot of weariness, sadness, and sometimes even anger and arguing. When I contrast this with what I see when our congregation is gathered for our Sunday evening services, I observe something very different. Faces are lifted in praise to God. I hear life stories of people who are changing; moving from darkness to light. The Lord is healing people physically, and helping them overcome depression, fear, addictive behaviour and suicidal thoughts. Nothing can melt a cold or indifferent heart like seeing the Spirit of God move among his people as they worship the Lord together.

Encouraging someone to regularly attend church is one of the best things a discipler can do for the people they are seeking to help. Both Jesus and the apostle Paul modelled this for us as we read first in Luke 4:16:

> Jesus travelled to Nazareth, where he had grown up. On the Sabbath day he went to the synagogue, as he always did, and stood up to read.

And then in Acts 17:1–2:

> Paul and Silas travelled through Amphipolis and Apollonia and came to Thessalonica

> where there was a synagogue. Paul went into the synagogue as he always did, and on each Sabbath day for three weeks, he talked with his fellow Jews about the Scriptures.

If Jesus and Paul made it their custom to attend the synagogue on the Sabbath, we should give the same attention to attending church as they did to attending the synagogue.

Billy Graham hit the nail on the head when he said, "Christ loved the Church and gave Himself for it. If our Lord loved it enough to die for it, then we should respect it enough to support and attend it."[38]

If we say we are too busy to attend every week, then we are too busy – or have our priorities wrong. Jesus was busy; he was about his Father's business, but he made worshipping in his Father's house a priority.

When we discover, if we haven't already, that church is more for the lost than the saved, we will find it a pleasure and delight to serve the lost there who don't know him yet. If we aren't at church, we aren't available to be a friend to those who need it most. Finding direction for our lives is always best discovered when we seek to serve others before ourselves. Attending church weekly, worshipping God, serving others, and growing in our discipleship will ensure that we are heading in the right direction. If we fail to attend church regularly, there is a certain guarantee that we will lose good direction on life's journey.

TEN

SETTING THE BAR

Bᴜᴛ ᴀs ᴄʀᴇᴀᴛᴜʀᴇs, ᴡᴇ ᴡɪʟʟ ɴᴇᴠᴇʀ be the Creator. God doesn't want you to become a god; he wants you to become godly – taking on his values, attitudes, and character. We are meant to "take on an entirely new way of life – a God-fashioned life, a life renewed from the inside and working itself into your conduct as God accurately reproduces his character in you."[39]

Get action. Seize the moment. Man was never intended to become an oyster.

Theodore Roosevelt[40]

Follow my example, as I follow the example of Christ.

Apostle Paul, 1 Corinthians 11:1

Several years ago, I started baking cakes. Not something every father of four boys does, but the church we attended

113

then was having a bake sale and Ruth was asked to supply a cake for it. She doesn't enjoy baking, hence she did what most wise wives would do: she asked her husband to do it. I didn't know much about baking, so I read one of Ruth's cookbooks on the subject. I discovered a handy hint which has been the secret to the success of my oft-praised Victoria sponge cakes. It is simple, but profound – a sponge cake mixture will never rise above the sides of the pan it is put in. If it is flat, heavy cakes you want, put them in a short pan, but if you want to bake a light, airy cake, you have to put it in a tall pan.

Callum is a young guy I disciple. He is passionate for Jesus, but in the past he had struggled to maintain a daily devotional time of prayer and Bible reading. I asked him if he would share with you about how my setting the bar high for him has given him the challenge of discipleship he really needed. He shares his story here:

> Throughout my Christian faith, one of the aspects that has been missing is reading the Bible regularly and without fail. When I was younger, I found it hard to read books. Every book I started, I would read half way through and give up. Therefore reading the Bible was always going to be tough. It got to a stage where I knew that God was really challenging me to read more and explore the Word further in my life, so I brought it up in mentoring.
>
> James and I had a think and a pray, and the next week we decided to read 1 Samuel. The James and James

Bible Study Facebook Group was created.[2] The only premise was that we were expected to read a chapter – which quickly turned into three – each day, from three different books of the Bible. We read one chapter from an Old Testament book, one from Psalms or Proverbs and one from a New Testament book. To keep each other accountable to reading every day, we posted our comments and feedback online. This enabled me not only to read the Bible daily, but also to get theological insight from my mentor.

To keep this level and amount of reading up has been a real challenge. Some days I'd wake up and have a large amount of apathy towards reading. Other days I would be out of the house from 6am to 8pm with little time to think, let alone read. The worst days were those where I'd messed up and felt ashamed about some sin I had committed that day.

However, I feel that if I wasn't challenged by James to read my Bible every day, I wouldn't have done it. If James was more relaxed and said, "You can do this if you want to" then I would definitely have made up excuses not to have done it.

This season of daily reading has been really rewarding. Taking time out to get to know God in a more intimate way by reading his Word has enabled me to live in his grace more, knowing that whatever I do, I am loved. Being pushed to read has increased my obedience, knowledge and understanding, and ultimately my love for the Word.

---

2   Callum's surname is James, hence, the James and James Facebook group

Setting the bar high for reading the Bible daily was the best thing I could have done for Callum. He has found it a bit of a challenge at times, but his efforts to keep going have really helped him in his Bible reading and how he applies the Word he is reading to his life.

Callum and I have had some great discussions about the Bible and the things we are learning from the passages of Scripture we are reading. How different things would be if I had settled for a low expectation that Callum only read his Bible when he felt like it.

Discipleship is about challenge to be better and to do better, which is something we really emphasise at regeneration. We didn't realise how much of a key feature that was for us until we had a group of South African pastors come and visit regen to gain an understanding of how we 'do church'. They spoke to our young people and listened to how we set the bar high for discipleship. One of the pastors commented that "At regeneration, mentoring is about total acceptance and total challenge". That was encouraging for us to hear.

If we set the bar low for the people we disciple, guess how much spiritual growth is going to happen in their lives? Not much. If we set the bar high, great opportunities for challenge and growth are more likely to happen. If we encourage people to read their Bible and pray every day – if we expect them to – they probably will. If we expect disciples to engage with their non-Christian friends, they most likely will. Referencing George Bush's phrase, "The soft bigotry of low expectations", Tavis Smiley offered: "If you don't expect them [students] to learn, if you don't expect them to succeed – then it becomes a self-fulfilling prophecy."[41]

Any dead fish can float downstream. I'm mixing metaphors here, but if we want to see people growing, we will expect them to take on the challenge of doing hard things. Resisting the temptation to get drunk, or have sex outside of marriage, or viewing pornography can be really hard when the expectation of non-believers can be a polar opposite.

Back in 2005, two teenage brothers named Alex and Brett Harris started what they call a "Rebelution". They became excited about a big idea; they saw young people were being badly underestimated. The brothers believed a whole generation had bought into a culture of low expectations. They came up with a plan, and then invited other young people and their parents to join in. They started a blog and began engaging with their generation around the globe. Their website has exceeded thirty-five million hits with a message of passion and creativity to challenge a generation to get out and do hard things. Alex and Brett had a plan. It was a 'setting the bar high' kind of plan and they stuck with it.

It is imperative to set the bar high for those you disciple, not just in the moral sense, but in the challenge to do great things for God. Encourage them to take risks in mission or stepping out to lead.

Ben, a young man from our congregation, shares his story of how being challenged really helped him to change in a significant way:

> For the past five years of my life, I have struggled with what many people, myself included, would term as 'overthinking'. Put simply, there are two defining points. Firstly, I found myself rarely having that 'headspace' (and that peace) to just be still; I was constantly thinking about things I needed to do, or to make decisions about. Secondly, I developed a habit of over analysing certain situations. For anyone who knows what this is like, you'll know that it causes you to feel like you're constantly spinning around in a tornado of thoughts, feelings and emotions. The truth begins to appear relative, feelings begin to cloud your judgement, emotions and the opinions of others become mountains … and it goes on. You never really feel peace; you often find yourself doubting God's truth and the devil begins to really mess with your emotions. So for me on a daily basis, this overthinking has meant that I've struggled to not only make time for God in prayer, but I've also struggled to feel connected to God.
>
> The Bible says that the enemy loves to attack God's people (John 10:10). God is the complete opposite of this – He is a God of peace, not of confusion (1 Corinthians 14:33). So when I chatted to my mentor,, about my struggles, we knew that I needed to really strip back all the clutter that would make

addressing this stumbling block otherwise impossible.
He suggested that I simply spend fifteen minutes
every day intentionally resting in God's presence,
without asking for anything. No overthinking, just
worshipping. To be honest, I was sceptical at first that
nothing would change, and even this felt like a tall
order to commit to. But I'm grateful that my mentor
encouraged me to make this a daily discipline.
Practically for me, implementing this wasn't easy, but
it meant purposefully coming to meet with God and
pouring out my heart in worship to him. I spent time
focusing on who God is, and understanding his vast,
extravagant love and grace. This changed the focus of
my heart entirely, and allowed me to press in to
prayer more freely. Prayer didn't feel like a chore in
that moment. It felt like a natural adoration of my
Father in the context of my relationship with him. It
also deepened my intimacy with him, and I no longer
felt overwhelmed all the time.

Through this process of challenge, I have realised that
I have lived with an orphan heart for many years. I
never fully understood how loved I was by the Father,
which in turn created a barrier in my relationship
with God. Now, even when I feel busy or distant
from God, this place of worship is where I come back
to. I continue to discover him.

Thank God we don't have to muddle through on our own.
Disciplers can really help people like Ben to see things
from a different perspective and can set some challenges
that will help to get them back on track or on the right
track, as was the case with Ben. His overthinking was

distracting him from his real purpose of worshipping God and not trying to figure everything out in his own strength. Although Ben was sceptical at first and didn't find it easy to take his mentor's advice, in the end he found a deeper intimacy with the Father that he wouldn't have known otherwise.

Inspire and expect people to do the necessary and sometimes hard things Kingdom living demands and you will see people rising to the challenge of a life lived for Christ – what an adventure it is.

ELEVEN

FINDING THE RHYTHMS OF GRACE

Rome wasn't built in a day.

Anon

Are you tired? Worn out? Burned out on religion? Come to me. Get away with me and you'll recover your life. I'll show you how to take a real rest. Walk with me and work with me–watch how I do it. Learn the unforced rhythms of grace. I won't lay anything heavy or ill-fitting on you. Keep company with me and you'll learn to live freely and lightly.

Jesus, Matthew 11:28–30 (The Message)

OUR CRAZY DOG, HUCK, HASN'T been trained to walk on a leash yet, so taking him for a stroll is pretty hard going for both of us. He strains on his leash so hard it causes him to gasp and wheeze like somebody having an asthma attack. It is uncomfortable for me to be pulled along in this way and it definitely looks ridiculous. I sometimes think how easy walking with Huck would be if I had a skateboard – we would both go everywhere very fast.

Getting pace right and finding the perfect balance between challenge and accepting the slow, seemingly non-existent pace of change or even resistance to the discipleship process isn't always easy, but to err with extra grace and heaps of love will always be a win. This will mean that we will need to be consistent in the inconsistencies. At times, I have become exasperated at the slow change I sometimes see in those I disciple or mentor, but I have to remind myself that I didn't get where I am spiritually overnight. My spiritual growth has been painfully slow at times. It doesn't hurt to take a good hard look in the mirror and remind ourselves of how patient God and others have been with us in our spiritual journey to maturity.

It is a wonderful thing to see change in the lives of those we seek to help, especially when the journey with them has been challenging at times. Rebecca shares her story of change in the discipleship process:

> I didn't grow up in a Christian family, but despite this, I attended a Christian school since I was eight years old. This gave me an interesting 'assumed' faith, based on my educational environment, but it didn't reconcile with my home life. I took my faith seriously, although I wouldn't say it changed areas of my life. The usual sins attractive to a teenager had never appealed to me, so it felt easy to consider myself to be a relatively good Christian – no drugs, boys, drink or wild parties. However, what was lacking was openness

about my struggles or recognition of my need or ability to change. This left me with a lot of emotional issues and baggage that I battled with, at times, on a daily basis. I also lacked a proper revelation of God's love for me.

Alongside this, I had great support from my Christian friends, and from my family as well. It was a blessing that they supported my fledgling faith despite not agreeing with it. However, there was still a big gaping hole where my faith wasn't growing. I believe this [was] because of a lack of challenge in my life.

The church I attended in my later teens was an amazing, Spirit-filled church, but even the leaders didn't appear to be discipled or open about their own lives – proven by photos on Facebook or fuelled by rumours I'd hear. I also had advice from my mum along the lines that no one needed to know my business, I shouldn't feel that I [had] to do anything or change, and I could be my own person. From a secular perspective, this was loving advice, but from a biblical standpoint, this attitude to discipleship doesn't sit well.

When I joined regeneration, I was offered mentoring, especially as I was dating James' son. The idea of this made me very uncomfortable – I believed I would be judged and thought everyone just wanted to know my personal business. My understanding of discipleship started to change when I was challenged about the danger of unconfessed sin. I had never realised that a lack of confession and my demands for extreme privacy as a Christian were not my right and that these attitudes were an obstacle in my walk with God. The Bible makes it clear that we have to be open about who we are – about our struggles and our besetting sins.

> So if we say we have fellowship with God, but we continue living in darkness, we are liars and do not follow the truth. But if we live in the light, as God is in the light, we can share fellowship with each other. Then the blood of Jesus, God's Son, cleanses us from every sin. If we say we have no sin, we are fooling ourselves, and the truth is not in us.
>
> 1 John 1:6–8

I began mentoring with James' wife, Ruth, who is now my mother-in-law. She has been very gracious and understanding with me. She allowed the time in our relationship to build up trust so I could be increasingly open. While absolutely challenging, Ruth was never judgemental. By her being such a great mentor, I started seeing rapid change in my life, with one particular year seeing me rid of multiple deep-rooted, life-long emotional issues. Through the discipleship process, Jesus has set me free from many battles. Seeing the fruit of discipleship allowed me to be really open and honest with Ruth. I'd rather her know everything so we can work through it together than struggle on my own.

I have been in mentoring for over five years now and never knew so much personal and spiritual growth was possible. Others have said I'm an unrecognisable person, and I feel that way. Mentoring isn't a comfortable process, but it is an essential one for anyone serious about their journey with God. When we put God above our own sensitivity and pride, we'll see genuine transformation in our lives in becoming more like Christ.

If we have the advantage of a few years' or even a few months' experience over someone we disciple or mentor, it can be tempting to be expecting too much of them regarding their spiritual growth. Ruth allowed time for Rebecca to change. Trust was needed and that took time, but it paid off in the end as Rebecca was able to open up more and find the change she was longing for.

People we disciple may not be ready to accept a suggestion or piece of advice we have to offer. The apostle Paul had to bear with the Corinthians because of their immaturity. He told them the plain facts:

> The teaching I gave you was like milk, not solid food, because you were not able to take solid food. And even now you are not ready.
>
> 1 Corinthians 3:2

But this was not before he had reminded them of his thanksgiving for the grace they had received from Jesus:

> I always thank my God for you because of the grace God has given you in Christ Jesus.
>
> 1 Corinthians 1:4

At the end of the letter, he warmly encouraged them:

> Be alert. Continue strong in the faith. Have courage,
> and be strong. Do everything in love.

1 Corinthians 16:13–14

Paul was speaking from a place of humility when he wrote those words. He knew how merciful Jesus was towards him when he was living against God. A prophecy in the book of Isaiah concerning Christ shows us the great compassion and longsuffering of Jesus towards those who may have a weak or diminishing faith in him.

> He will not break a bent twig. He will not put out
> a dimly burning flame. He will be faithful and make
> everything right.

Isaiah 42:3 (NIRV)

Jesus' attitude and behaviour towards these kinds of people gives us a good example of how to disciple others well. Everything we do in discipling others should be done with great love.

Paul's attitude towards the Corinthians was also a model example of how to treat people in a mentoring relationship. Love must be the goal – always. If we aren't discipling people with the "unforced rhythms of grace" and sacrificial love, we shouldn't be discipling anyone.

TWELVE

GOING DEEPER

Look beneath the surface so you can judge correctly.

Jesus, John 7:24 (NLT)

To be loved but not known is comforting but super-ficial. To be known and not loved is our greatest fear. But to be fully known and truly loved is, well, a lot like being loved by God. It is what we need more than anything. It liberates us from pretence, humbles us out of our self-righteousness, and fortifies us for any difficulty life can throw at us.

Timothy Keller[42]

PEOPLE LEARN BEST BY DOING, or not doing as the case may be, e.g. homework not handed in on time, job assignments not completed at work by a given deadline, or by simply grabbing a cat by the tail. By doing the latter, you will receive a swift and unpleasant education and you may also come to know what cat scratch fever is. I have had it and it isn't pleasant. Funnily enough, I contracted a case of it from one of my sisters, but that is another story.

Needless to say, the consequences of our actions or inactions give us ample opportunity to learn from our mistakes – if we let them. It's tempting to judge people and think, "If they would only listen to my advice, everything would go so much better for them." You may think your solution to his or her problem may be as easy as falling off a log, but it might prove something of a challenge for them. The old Native American proverb still applies today, "Don't judge a man until you've walked a mile in his moccasins." Grace and patience are required – sometimes in liberal amounts. If someone is struggling with insomnia, it is no use suggesting they drink warm milk and read a boring book before bed if they are being kept awake by thoughts they might be fired from their job, lose their home or go bankrupt. It will be pointless to suggest someone with an eating disorder eat three square meals a day. Presenting problems abound. Always think deeper. Go deeper.

If you find it difficult to get to the root of a besetting sin or problem, it is always helpful to pray and ask the Lord, "What is the root cause of this? Is this the real problem, or is this issue a result of something else?" The person you are seeking to help may or may not be aware there is a deeper, more profound reason for the problem they face. This is why we need the sensitivity of the Holy Spirit to guide us.

A young woman from our church attended a series we were running at our Bible study, taken from the book *Emotionally Healthy Spirituality* by Peter Scazzero. [43]

Anne-Marie explains in her own words how attending the series affected her:

> Realising that you are a hardened and unmoving person is one of the most detrimental things to your relationship with a loving God. From my teenage years up until my early twenties, I sometimes felt a disconnect from people. I didn't find joy in sharing any part of myself and so my friendships were very shallow. This in itself was not the problem, but during the Emotionally Healthy Church series, God instead asked why I was so comfortable with shallow relationships.

> The answer was not because I was shy, although shyness had always been the reason why others thought I wouldn't open up. Truly, it was because of deep hurts that prevented me from going deeper.

> The deep hurts had come in many ways. The most prevalent was allowing words of discouragement to take root. People I should have trusted would speak so little of me. They would go out of their way to make me feel small. During a very impressionable time in my life, I internalised many of these words spoken against my character. Despite putting on a mask of "I'm OK", those words secretly festered and I formed a very low opinion of myself. It went deeper than self-esteem; I felt that I was innately useless, with no voice. For years to come, I would let people in, but only so far.

Someone once said to me, "Anne-Marie, you have allowed me to get to know the particulars of your life (name, age, family, hobbies), but why won't you let me know you deeper?" I just did not understand what this meant. This was said three years before the series. During the initial stages of the series, I had a picture in a dream. It was of a heart that was tangled in several layers of barbed wire, the prongs of which pierced the flesh of the heart. As I listened to the series, I realised that God was showing me a picture of my heart and the barbed wire represented all the little hurts that had reached the 'heart' of me and were now surfacing. I remember breaking down and telling God that there was a reason I didn't want to take the hurts out. I would be left with a damaged heart, full of holes. Surely a 'guarded' heart was better that a 'weepy' one. I didn't want to be that woman with a weak, clichéd sob story. He reminded me that he loves me, and because he loves me, he wants me to be whole. His greatest desire is for me to be whole. This meant dealing with the root of the problem; overcoming the power of the past. My moment of breakthrough came when the pastor shared a scripture during one of the talks. The scripture was EXACTLY what God had been saying all along; I had never seen it before:

I will give you a new heart and put a new spirit in you; I will remove from you your heart of stone and give you a heart of flesh.

Ezekiel 36:26 (NIVUK)

A heart of flesh. This was what God wanted for me; he needed me to have a heart of flesh so that I can love and be loved. That night I wrote in my journal: "Heal my heart. Where there are holes, there is his healing. The barbed wire of my past can't hold me. I am new." For years prior to this revelation, I hid because it was just much easier. Since this outpouring of healing during the series, I have not felt the burden of past discouragements; I know who am I and my voice is important. I know I am loved deeply and I have learned that guarding your heart in Christ is different than barricading it for fear of dealing with the issue. Once God highlighted this in me, he placed opportunities for me to exercise this healing. I had to 'walk the walk'. For a long time, opening up was the struggle. If there was a problem, I would carry it, bury it and pretend that it didn't matter. The Emotionally Healthy Church series challenged me to go deeper within my past but God also presented new challenges that would seal it in my future. He brought people into my life who asked me to speak up about what God had been doing. At first, I wanted to skim the surface and revert back to old ways. There were times where I thought I was being open, but really I was speaking about the surface things. I had to speak from the deeper healing I had received! I am so grateful for those who would continually speak truths about openness and transparency. Their challenge helped to push God's healing to completion.

As I stepped out in obedience, God met me every time. Through his Word and through his people, he confirmed and reaffirmed that there was a real danger in staying quiet, or worse, speaking around an issue; saying a lot but not really saying anything at all.

Thankfully, I now have friends that are as close as siblings and I was able to root out a lot of other issues because I could trust God to go there. The Emotionally Healthy Church series was truly the catalyst for everything God has done in me. He was always in the habit of blessing me and I have always appreciated it, but there was something so powerful in accepting – really accepting – that he loves me. There is such a freedom in being open and transparent, not only for my good but also for the good of my relationships. I was born to be a communicator of God's love; how could I do this when I struggled to be open?

I am confident and proud of the journey I have been on because I am loved by God, who is intimately interested in the root of the problem. He didn't want me to be proud and defensive, but vulnerable and whole.

Anne-Marie's shyness was hiding the deeper issue of not understanding who she was in Christ and how much God loved her. Shyness wasn't the real root of what was holding her back from becoming a whole person. Breaking the power of the past requires that we go deeper into our lives and not make excuses or put up façades to hide who we really are. Anne-Marie's friend challenged her about her lack of transparency, but she wasn't ready and didn't even comprehend the fact that she wasn't being open. It took three years before she would open the door to vulnerability. We can't rush people into 'opening up' until they are ready, but we can certainly ask questions to get them thinking.

In our personal journeys of discipleship, there will be times when we don't fully understand what a discipler or mentor is teaching us, or why they may be asking particular questions. When told by a heavenly angel things that were too hard for her to grasp, Jesus' mother Mary simply pondered on what the angel said:

> But Mary was keeping within herself all these things (sayings), weighing *and* pondering them in her heart.

> Luke 2:19 (AMPC)

This is not to say that everything you hear from a friend is equivalent to the message of angels – sometimes it may be far from it. But we can always weigh up what we are hearing to know whether or not it is God speaking though that person or if it is just a blessed thought on their part:

> What are heavy? sea-sand and sorrow.
> What are brief? today and tomorrow.
> What are frail? spring blossoms and youth.
> What are deep? the ocean and truth.

> Christina Rossetti[44]

Truth about ourselves is found in the depths of who we are, not in the shallows of generic pleasantries. Don't be afraid to go to the deep places. The truth is there.

THIRTEEN

ENCOURAGEMENT
DOES MORE

And so we are transfigured much like the Messiah,
our lives gradually becoming brighter and more
beautiful as God enters our lives and we become like
him.

2 Corinthians 3:18 (The Message)

Correction does much, but encouragement does
more.

Johann Wolfgang von Goethe[45]

I TRAVELLED TO A HEALING RETREAT to see someone I
value greatly for her loving insight. Irrational fears were
plaguing me and were causing me to have terrible panic
attacks. I felt so weak and helpless at this time and had low
self-esteem as a result. I was taken aback when she turned
to the person next to her and commented on how courageous and brave I was in the face of the panic attacks. Me?

Courageous? It appeared to me to be the furthest thing from the truth, but when I thought about it, she was right. I wasn't running from my fears, even though they were plaguing my every waking moment; I was acknowledging they were there and I was taking steps to get help, even though I was quite fearful in the process.

Hearing those affirming words that day encouraged me so much. The panic attacks have diminished and weakened over the years, which has been a testimony to the healing power of God at work in my life. It is great to have friends who find ways to encourage us in the hard times and who give hope that irrational fears will be conquered in Jesus' name.

In our discipling of others, we should never lead them to believe the Christian life is a long list of dos and don'ts, or a series of hoops to jump through. Jumping through hoops is for circus animals, not for God's children. As I mentioned earlier, grace and patience are needed in many mentoring relationships, but equally important are liberal doses of praise and affirmation. Brennan Manning gives great wisdom about this:

> To affirm a person is to see the good in them that they cannot see in themselves and to repeat it in spite of appearances to the contrary. Please, this is not some Pollyanna optimism that is blind to the reality of evil, but rather like a fine radar system that is tuned in to the true, the good, and the beautiful.[46]

There might be times when it may seem hard to find something to give affirmation to when people we mentor struggle to make headway, but with the help of the Holy Spirit, we will find it. The simple fact someone is choosing to meet with us is cause for warm praise and celebration. It is wonderful they are accepting the challenge to grow into the image of Christ.

Sometimes we need to state the obvious good things we see in others because it may only be obvious to ourselves and may be completely missed by the person who really needs a word of encouragement. I think sometimes people reckon that since I am a minister and have been a Christian for such a long time that I don't need to be encouraged. The fact is, I need it just as much as the next person. Never underestimate the importance of encouraging others, we are all on a journey.

There are so many ways we can give people encouragement. We can do so face-to-face, by email, letter, card, text, Facebook message, Twitter – you get the idea. Whatever you do, try to make it memorable and think about what you would like to say beforehand. It really can make a difference to someone's day, and even to their life. Besides face-to-face encouragement, most of the other kinds can be saved so that when someone is feeling low they can reread the message and be encouraged all over again. Ruth and I keep a folder of encouragements we have been given over the years. It is always uplifting to read the positive things people have said to us, and it keeps us going when things get tough.

Why not make a start today by giving someone some memorable encouragement they really could use? It doesn't really cost anything to do, but the reward of seeing someone's face brighten is worth its weight in gold.

FOURTEEN

GET OVER IT

I'm not running around as a continual ray of sunshine. It's just I don't believe in wasting time feeling sorry for myself. Get over it.

Aimee Mullins[47]

No, dear brothers and sisters, I have not achieved it, but I focus on this one thing: Forgetting the past and looking forward to what lies ahead, I press on to reach the end of the race and receive the heavenly prize for which God, through Christ Jesus, is calling us.

Philippians 3:13–14 (NLT)

AFTER WE HAVE FINISHED A TALK at regen, we offer an opportunity for people to respond to the message and a reminder that people can receive prayer ministry during the worship. Once, I was going through the usual spiel and said something I had never said before; I may have thought it, but I had never said it. "Get over it." Did I say that out loud? My gut instinct was that it was the right thing to say then, but at the same time I worried it might be misconstrued. It sounded so pastorally uncouth. Who tells people to get over anything when they are making an appeal for people to receive prayer in a church service? What I actually said was, "We offer prayer ministry at the back and you may feel embarrassed or too frightened to get prayer, but [there was a slight pause here] you have to get over it."

Sometimes people need a gentle push in the right direction. Something which will wake them up to the possibility that there is more to life, and if they take a risk – a little risk – God will meet with them in ways they may never have imagined. That phrase has worked its way into the regen vocabulary because people have come to realise it is full of truth. We have so much to gain by letting go of and getting healed from the hurts of the past. It opens up doors of endless possibility to know we don't have to be held as slaves to the bad experiences of our lives.

I was talking to a young woman at one of our residentials in Derbyshire and she remarked in the course of our conversation that the first thing she heard in the morning, via her alarm clock, was "Get over it." I thought I had misheard so I asked her later what she meant. She said she had recorded those words in her phone and set them as

her alarm to wake her to those three words of encouragement. Itty tells the story in her own words:

> It was almost like someone pouring a cold bucket of
> water over you while you're still in bed. When I heard
> those words "get over it", I was shocked. How could I
> just 'get over' my issues? How could things be that
> simple? Those questions sparked off a conversation
> with God that would keep going to this day. As James
> continued to share what was on his heart, I felt God
> highlight some areas in my life that he wanted me to
> close the door on. Some of these things seemed small,
> like mild annoyances or inconveniences in my life.
> But other areas were huge, and my failure to
> surrender them to God and move past them meant
> that I had been carrying shame, fear and guilt for
> years.
>
> While James was speaking, I realised that I had to do
> something, and respond to what God was asking me
> to do. I needed to remind myself each day to "remove
> from our lives anything that would get in the way and
> the sin that so easily holds us back" (Hebrews 12:1).
> I went home that night and set my alarm to play the
> words "get over it" every time I woke up. And each
> day I grew more and more in perseverance and focus!
> What started out as a shock to the system suddenly
> became the biggest encouragement for my season of
> personal growth.

There are times when we will have to encourage people
like Itty to get over problems they may never have enter-
tained getting over. They may have done things in the past

that have hurt others or themselves. This sounds scandalous. How could we do that?

I once attended a special church service to hear a remarkable woman called Jackie Pullinger. She is a missionary based in Hong Kong who works among thieves, prostitutes, murderers, drug dealers and brutal Chinese triad gangs. I went to a church in London to hear her speak. She said something that night that startled me a bit: "For the Christian, there can be no regret." No regret? "How can that be true?" I asked myself, but after thinking about it, I realised that it is, of course, quite true.

Why did I find such a statement so startling? I shouldn't have, since this is essentially what the gospel is about. God, through the finished work of Jesus on the cross, makes everything right; our mistakes, sins, failures – everything. He miraculously manages to turn our bad choices and failures into good by his mercy and love. This is the scandal of grace, the scandal of the amazing cross of Christ. God wants us to get over our past, to move on with him into a new way of living by the healing power of the Holy Spirit, and he wants us to lovingly encourage others to do the same.

I recently asked Itty to share her testimony at regen. She shared these powerful words with the congregation:

> It started with the alarm, but as I began to enter the process of healing, I found that

I could only shut the door on some things by revisiting them, and finally surrendering their effects and consequences to God. It was definitely the most painful thing I've done, almost like pulling out some broken glass, but once I had the chance to turn around and look at the actual things that shaped my life, that made me who I was, I could finally say goodbye. I find that when we just run away from things, we don't really shut the door. Sometimes we have to turn back, close the door, and then we get to walk away freely.

Living the life of freedom God has called us to live will mean getting over things just like Itty did. Getting over things leads to getting on with living the life the Lord has for us, and that is exactly what we are going to look at in the next chapter.

FIFTEEN

CALLING OUT DESTINY

When you become an instrument in God's hands as He transfers someone from the realm of darkness into the kingdom of His Son, you make a difference in the person's eternal destiny. Not only that, but Satan also receives a devastating blow.

Charles Stanley[48]

The lowest form of discipling is policing sin. The highest form is calling out destiny.

Anon

THE LORD HAS PLANS FOR his people. We read about them throughout the Bible. In Psalm 138:8, King David confidently asserts, "The LORD will work out his plans for my life – for your faithful love, O LORD, endures forever" (NLT). Confident in the Lord's love, David acknowledges that the Lord has a purpose for his life. In several of Paul's epistles to the New Testament Church, he begins his opening greetings with phrases similar to this, "Paul, called to be an apostle of Christ Jesus by the will of God." In 1 Timothy 1:1, he makes a similar claim, "Paul, an apostle of Christ Jesus by the command of God our Saviour and of Christ Jesus our hope" (NIVUK). He leaves no room for doubt in his writings – his calling is nothing but the will and command of God.

There are Christians who believe there is no will of God. They believe what happens in the Christian life is down to personal choice. Scripture does not bear this out. Many times in the Bible, we are admonished to seek out the will of God for our lives. This doesn't mean what to have for breakfast: porridge or cornflakes? Rather, it is about seeking God's will concerning what is on his heart – doing what is just, loving mercy and walking humbly with him. Check out Micah 6:8.

How can we align our wills and desires with God's so we can fully reflect the glory of God through our education, career and relationship choices? The devil will try his best to get people off track. He will try to isolate them and cause them to think they can't do anything great for God. These are lies. We each play a part as the body of Christ in combating them. In Proverbs 11:14, the warning and admonition is clear: "Where there is no guidance the people fall, But in abundance of counselors there is victory" (NASB). As the people of God – as a community of believers – it is our duty to watch over one another in love.

The apostle Paul speaks from experience in his great epistle to the Romans:

> Don't copy the behaviour and customs of this world, but let God transform you into a new person by changing the way you think. Then you will learn to know God's will for you, which is good and pleasing and perfect.

> Romans 12:2 (NLT)

Paul heard the message by direct intervention from Jesus himself on the road to Damascus. The majority of us will not have a glorious revelation from God like Paul did, but God will have spoken to us in some way. Through study of the Bible and prayer, and with the help of Christian friends, we can discover what great things the Lord is asking us to do for the sake of his Kingdom.

I shared earlier how in a season of unemployment I learned God's will for me by simply letting another person speak into my life. The greengrocer's suggestion that I work with elderly people in the care industry, and the words of 2 Thessalonians 3:10 – "Anyone who refuses to work should not eat" – were straightforward enough for me to understand. The choices I made back then have led me to where I am now. They informed my destiny.

Writing this book is a result of me seeking out the will of God. On 19 August 2008, at the Soul Survivor summer festival in Shepton Mallet, I wrote the following in my diary concerning my desire to write a book:

> I had a little "heart to heart" with God about the book in the Big Top this morning. I keep thinking about it – a bit too much. I have too many ideas about what could go in, and then I think there's not enough. I've been thinking of asking Jen [a writer I happen to be friends with] about this. I've prayed and told God I won't mention the idea to anyone. If he wants me to do it, I need strong confirmation. At the close of the meeting, Mike [Pilavachi] prayed that God would "give us the keys to unlock the doors of people's hearts". That is my prayer too. Although these words are encouraging, I need something more specific.

After a whole year of telling no one except Ruth about my desire to write, I attended a prophecy session at the same festival the following summer. A woman who didn't know me at all spoke these words over me:

> I don't know if you actually like to write at all, but I've got the sense that you've got a real story to tell; that your past, there's a real history there, and that is something that God is really interested in and he's going to really use for his glory.

Needless to say, I was overwhelmed that God spoke so directly and clearly to me about my heart's desire to write. Granted, I had to wait a whole year for the answer, but when he did answer there was no doubt that I should begin writing. God used a woman who didn't know me at all to relay a very special word of encouragement to me. This is a gift of prophecy. The specific word given to me is called a word of knowledge:

In Pentecostal and charismatic understanding, the word of knowledge is frequently defined as the ability of a person to know what God is currently doing or intends to do in the life of another person. It can also be understood as knowing the secrets of another person's heart. Through this revelation, it is believed that the Lord encourages the faith of the believer to receive the healing or comfort the Holy Spirit offers.

God uses prophecy throughout the Bible to call and direct people and nations into his will for them. We must position ourselves to receive what our loving God has for us. One of the best ways to help others do this is to find out what God has spoken to them already by way of his Word and/or personal prophecy. They may have been given words of knowledge and then do nothing about them for lack of faith, unbelief or maybe even fear.

Ruth and I once visited a vicar who had a special gift of prophecy and discernment. We had travelled about an hour to meet him at his church in Kent. I was looking forward to receiving prayer and maybe even a prophetic word from him. He prayed for me first and simply said, "Lord, I pray James will do what you have already asked him to do." He then prayed and prophesied over Ruth for a considerably longer time than he had spent praying for me. I couldn't believe it. I had driven an hour to receive a word from the Lord and the only one given to me was that I was to do what God had already asked me to do. After getting over the initial disappointment of the word and its brevity, I came to realise it was the only word I needed to hear. God had already given me many words of direction and dreams to follow; all I needed to hear was, "Get on with it." If God has spoken specifically to you to do something, it is common sense to do it before seeking out any other words.

It is a wonderful privilege to journey with people, encouraging them to do what is impossible in the natural realm. We need to remind one another that God is the God of the impossible. Ask the person you are discipling to share any Bible verses or passages that have spoken to them about their future. If words of prophecy have been given, encourage them to share those as well. The following is some guidance in how to test words and Bible verses that may have been spoken over people:

A word of prophecy should align with Scripture

People can easily get deceived when they do not give proper attention to the Word. If a husband comes to me and says it is God's will for him to leave his wife and live with another woman, I will immediately know the word is not from God. There will be no need to pray about whether or not it is the Lord's will for that man to leave his wife. The Scriptures are clear on this matter. Committing adultery is a sin.

Personal prophecies are meant to strengthen, encourage and comfort people

> But those who prophesy are speaking to people to give them strength, encouragement, and comfort.

> 1 Corinthians 14:3

If someone has been given a word which doesn't fit with at least one of these three things, then it is simply not from God.

I'm a bit embarrassed to share this, but I'm certain it will help you to understand this point a bit better. I remember praying during a time of prayer and fasting. I had a strong impression martyrdom was awaiting me in South America. It plagued me for weeks. I believed it was a word from God. I didn't share it with anyone, but I eventually told Ruth and she dismissed it out of hand. It wasn't giving me any sense of peace and I was having obsessive thoughts about it. It wasn't a word which was strengthening, encouraging or comforting to me. I should have recognised from the outset it was not a true message from the Lord. Thank the Lord I had someone I could share that 'word' with. Satan's plan to steal my peace, make me fearful, and get me off track was thwarted.

Prophecies and Bible promises are conditional

Someone may have had words spoken to them about going to be a missionary to China, and this may have been confirmed through the Word, prayer and a whole host of other things, but if a person is not living a life that is honouring to God, it is unlikely they will ever step on Chinese soil. If they do happen to get there via their own striving, they will not have the blessing of God on it, since God will only commission and bless those who are living a life which is honouring to him.

Words and prophecies will have a certain ring of truth about them.

If something doesn't sit right about a word, it is best to let it settle. God is in no rush. If he wants to get a message across, he will make it very clear. There will be a sense of peace and quiet expectation over his word, not hype or muddled thinking. "God is not a God of confusion but a

God of peace" (1 Corinthians 14:33). When people chop and change what they want to do and have some new word or revelation every other week, it is a sign something is not right.

We should never act on one word or prophecy in isolation. Paul, in 2 Corinthians 13:1, reminds the Corinthians of the Old Testament law. He said, "I will come to you for the third time. "Every case must be proved by two or three witnesses." If God wants us to do something, he will confirm it by more than one word or prophecy. As I mentioned earlier, I waited for a whole year after sensing God wanted me to write a book. I kept seeking God's will in the matter. I only shared it with Ruth and I didn't strive to make it happen.

If appropriate, encourage people to have short, mid and long-term plans concerning their God-given dreams and destiny. Work together to find some focus and see what God will do as he leads you by his Word and his Spirit.

SIXTEEN

—

RESOLVING CONFLICT

Blessed are the peacemakers,
for they will be called children of God.

Jesus, Matthew 5:9 (NIVUK)

Conflict can and should be handled constructively;
when it is, relationships benefit. Conflict avoidance
is *not* the hallmark of a good relationship. On the
contrary, it is a symptom of serious problems and of
poor communication.

Harriet B. Braiker[49]

EVERYONE WILL HAVE TO DEAL with conflict at some
point in their lives. Job's friend Eliphaz stated the
obvious: "People produce trouble as surely as sparks fly
upward" (Job 5:7). There is no use hiding from conflict;
wherever you find people, you will find the potential for
it. The devil does his level best to bring discord and

disunity among people, especially in the Church. It is always best to have a management system in place to deal with it; something that will neutralise the potentially damaging effect conflict can have on us and others. There are healthy ways of dealing with conflict, but sadly many people operate in extremes; running away from it or running towards it like a cheetah after a gazelle. It may be a case of fight, flight, or sometimes sidestepping the issue. Churches that fail to deal with conflict can fast become pseudocommunities:

> Pseudocommunity is "an unconscious, gentle process whereby people who want to be loving attempt to be so by telling little white lies, by withholding some of the truth about themselves and their feelings in order to avoid conflict. Pseudocommunity is conflict-avoiding; true community is conflict-resolving."

> M. Scott Peck[50]

Avoiding conflict is as effective as trying to keep a beach ball under water; it will stay down for so long, only to pop up again. Far better to bring problem issues to the surface and allow them to be dealt with in a calm and constructive way. We have it in our power to be conflict-resolving. People who run from conflict may resent your involvement in trying to bring things out into the open, but this is the very thing God requires us to do, however unpopular it can make us. "Being a leader is like asking to be ugly"– so says

Mike Pilavachi from Soul Survivor.[51] We may not always be the most popular people if we seek to grasp the nettle of conflict, but we will have God's approval and blessing on us as we seek to guard against the Church becoming a pseudocommunity. This is a fair enough trade-off.

If people have issues with other people, or they know others have issues with them, it is always best for them to work out the problem with the other person. Telling everybody what "Joe or Jane did to us" may feel freeing and may enable us to vent a bit of frustration, but it will do nothing to resolve the problem. Only love and a great amount of grace will do that:

> So when you offer your gift to God at the altar, and you remember that your brother or sister has something against you, leave your gift there at the altar. Go and make peace with that person, and then come and offer your gift.

(Matthew 5:23–24)

Jesus stressed the importance of making peace with others because if we cannot have peace with them, it will not be possible to have peace with God, and peace with God should be the heart desire of every Christian.

The best way to deal with conflict with others is to have a personal conversation with the person. If that does not work, bring someone else into the situation that both parties can trust to be impartial, and loving in their wisdom and judgement. If these efforts fail, the Bible instructs us to bring unresolved conflict to the leaders of the church who can then mediate and help everyone find a way forward with love and grace.

The devil's aim is always to stir up strife and discord. God hates this:

> There are six things the LORD hates, seven that are detestable to him: haughty eyes, a lying tongue, hands that shed innocent blood, a heart that devises wicked schemes, feet that are quick to rush into evil, a false witness who pours out lies and a person who stirs up conflict in the community.

> Proverbs 6:16–19 (NIVUK)

Let's flip the proverb and consider the Lord will love the opposite of what he hates. So, the Lord will love humble eyes, a tongue that tells the truth, hands that heal, a heart that devises righteous schemes, feet that are quick to rush into goodness, and a true witness who pours out truth and who works for peace in the community.

Imagine a community of people doing the things the Lord loves. This is what the world is looking for, but sadly the last place many would think of looking would be the Church. Every one of us has the power to create a grace-filled community, and this is exactly what we are determined to do at regeneration.

SEVENTEEN

MENTORING AT REGEN

ENCOURAGING CORPORATE WORSHIP

Before we encourage anyone to enter into a mentoring or accountability partnership at regen, we ask them to be dedicated to the body of Christ by attending Sunday worship and midweek Bible study. This demonstrates commitment to the church and lets us know a person is serious about their discipleship. From time to time, we have people who come for a short while and want lots of prayer input and personal time, but they aren't interested in committing to the fundamentals of the Christian life, weekly corporate worship, serving, Bible study and prayer. We have a duty and obligation to God to use the church's financial and human resources responsibly. This is not possible if we don't use our time wisely with people who are not serious about their commitment to discipleship. Everyone is welcome to attend regen, whether or not they are part of a mentoring partnership, but we just cannot invest a lot of time mentoring people who won't help themselves in becoming the people Christ is calling them to be.

Commitment to attending church regularly is vital to spiritual growth for the individual, but there is another aspect of church attendance which is often overlooked. If a person is not regularly attending church, the community of believers will miss them. Each one of us has a unique mix of gifts and talents no one else on earth has; these things are a complement to the body of Christ. If we are sitting at home, how will the body of Christ be built up?

> You should not stay away from the church
> meetings, as some are doing, but you should
> meet together and encourage each other. Do
> this even more as you see the day coming.
>
> Hebrews 10:25

We need one another for encouragement, challenge and service, which leads on nicely to the next encouragement.

ENCOURAGING SERVING

Serving is a key indicator in our lives as to how serious we are about our faith and commitment to the body of Christ. Jesus' disciples had an argument among themselves as to who was the greatest. He had to point out something that was completely lost on them, despite the fact he had done life with them for three years. He plainly told them, "I am among you as one who serves" (Luke 22:27, NIVUK).

How his disciples failed to comprehend Jesus' humble mission of serving, beggars belief. He tirelessly travelled from place to place attending to the needs of the poor and dispossessed. His plans were often interrupted as people asked him to go and pray for beloved servants, sick relatives, or friends. He taught and fed 5,000 people, not including women and children, and he healed those who were ill among them immediately after the brutal beheading of his cousin John the Baptist. His original intention was to get away to a quiet place to grieve and pray over the loss of his cousin, but his servant heart was demonstrated by his selfless love in serving them first. He gave a visual aid to the disciples and us by serving others first as a priority over his own comfort and position.

When we offer ourselves as servants of God, we demonstrate the truth that we are the hands and feet of Christ. What a privilege and responsibility it is to be ambassadors for Christ in this way. We should never shy away from inviting the people we serve to this high calling. We've observed many times how serving engenders a sense of belonging at regen like nothing else ever could. Many years ago when one of our young leaders, was about eighteen, he got a vision of what a church would look like for young people his age. He grew up in a church that catered more for people aged sixty and above. At regen, he suggested ways of being Church that would resonate with his peers, he encouraged them to attend and he served like crazy to get our fledgling church off the ground. Those experiences gave him ample insight into what church for young people would and would not look like.

If you've never been involved in a church plant before, there is something you should know: starting new churches can be incredibly hard work. Our young leader believed in something more than he could see in his present situation, and he wasn't afraid to work for it. It wasn't difficult to get young people like him to serve because they had a vision of something bigger than themselves. They knew it wouldn't be easy and it would require arriving at church early for setting up and staying late for setting down. The joy that comes when people see non-believers coming into the Kingdom as a result of serving and witness is a wonderful thing.

When young people come to regen, they see our people serving joyfully without complaining. Our members have discovered Jesus words are true: "It is more blessed to give than to receive" (Acts 20:35).

Serving doesn't begin at membership. Serving can be an entry point to church. When we started our morning service, we served a cooked breakfast beforehand. Many of the homeless people who came along would help us set up even before they considered regen to be their church. There is something very special in feeling a sense of belonging to something bigger than yourself. We are part of God's family; we love to serve one another.

This is all a bit like breathing. If we don't take a breath in, we will faint. If we don't breathe out, we will also faint. This is parallel to serving. There are times when we need to receive from God and others, and there are times when we need to give to God and others. This is a healthy balance, which fosters dynamic spiritual growth in the heart of a believer.

ENCOURAGING PEOPLE TO COME UNDER THE AUTHORITY OF THE BIBLE

When the authority of the Bible is not taken as an absolute, anything goes. Rousseau said, "In the beginning, God created man in his own image. Man, being a gentleman, returned the favour."

When we want to know what God looks like, we look at Jesus. When we worship a God that looks anything different to Jesus, we are simply worshipping a god made in our own image. It is pointless to attempt to rewrite the Bible – to decide who God will and will not be. If we fail to take the Bible as the inspired Word of God, we open ourselves up to great error and needless pain.

Take for instance what sociologists Christian Smith and Melinda Lundquist Denton discovered in their research into a combination of dogmas held by American youth. As they investigated their common religious beliefs, they found many of the young people believed in a variety of moral statutes not exclusive to any particular world religion. Their label for the compound of statutes is Moralistic Therapeutic Deism. Here is a summary of what they found:

1. A god exists who created and ordered the world and watches over human life on earth.

2. God wants people to be good, nice, and fair to each other, as taught in the Bible and by most world religions.

3. The central goal of life is to be happy and to feel good about oneself.

4. God does not need to be particularly involved in one's life, except when God is needed to resolve a problem.

5. Good people go to heaven when they die.[52]

Although most people will never have heard of Moralistic Therapeutic Deism, most will recognise these commonly held beliefs. They are certainly not exclusive to American youth. I would venture to say if you were to ask almost anyone who happened to be walking down your local high street what kind of belief they had about religion – if they had any – it would probably bear a resemblance to the one above.

From a biblical standard, points one and two are true while the remaining three points are false. When people don't have a point of reference other than themselves, it allows for great error and bondage to self-imposed or man-made rules which draw them away from the simple message of grace through the finished work of Jesus on the cross.

When people pose questions like, "Did Adam and Eve exist?" the subtext is usually something along the lines of, "Can I have sex with my partner before getting married?" or, "Is it OK for me to cheat on my taxes?" We have to decide if we are going to come under the authority of Scripture, or if we intend to presume authority over Scripture. The authority of Scripture over our lives is paramount if we want to live the full life God intends for us.

The author Elisabeth Elliot got to the heart of the matter when she tackled people's doubts about biblical authority:

> This is the question we need to ask ourselves when we are seeking 'solutions' to our problems. Often we want only an audience. We want the chance to air grievances, to present our excuses, to make an explanation for our behavior, rather than a cure. More often than not the clearest and most direct answer can be found in the Word, but it must be sought honestly.
>
> > The way of the Lord gives refuge to the honest man, but dismays those who do evil.
> > *Proverbs 10:29 (NEB)*
>
> We can approach God's word with a will to obey whatever it says to us about our present situation, or

we can avoid it and say to anyone who would try to point us to it, "Don't throw the Book at me." The latter is an evasion, which supports our suspicion that our problems are, in fact, insoluble. The honest (i.e., humble) heart will indeed find the Lord's way to be a refuge.[53]

God hasn't left us without guidance in this life of ours. His primary way of speaking to us is by his Word. Let's not undervalue the riches of the Bible. Read it every day if you want to grow and be more like Jesus. This truth is sometimes so simple that we miss it if we aren't careful.

ENCOURAGING SURRENDER

The word 'surrender' sticks in the craw of many in our present age of entitlement, which is a shame because they are seriously missing the point of surrender. When we lay down our way of living in surrender, we are able to take up God's way, which is far better for us than we could ever imagine.

I have already spoken at length about this in Chapter 2. It is important to encourage surrender since it opens the gateway to God's holy way. Jesus showed us how we can surrender to the Father's will and do what he asks us to do. This is surrender and it brings peace and joy like nothing else can.

> So Jesus explained, "I tell you the truth, the
> Son can do nothing by himself. He does

only what he sees the Father doing.
Whatever the Father does, the Son also
does." *John 5:19 (NLT)*

The more we get to grips with this truth Jesus spoke of
and modelled, the greater our peace and joy will be.

In this story, Cassie shares how she was encouraged by
her mentor to fully surrender to God in forgiving her
father. It meant a struggle, but one which led to freedom:

Before December 2012, I had a lot of frustration and
anger towards my dad. I hadn't forgiven him for all
the times he had let me down, hurt me or not done
what I wanted him to do. I hadn't forgiven him
because he didn't know me. I noticed that when I met
up with him, I had lingering thoughts like "he doesn't
even really care for me" and "he doesn't really know
who the real Cassie is".

When these thoughts became more regular, I decided
I needed to get prayer. I went to Naomi and
explained to her how I felt about my dad and we
prayed that God would help me forgive him. I went
to Naomi for prayer a few times, but I was still feeling
frustration and anger towards Dad. I didn't feel any
different towards him; I still felt really let down by
him.

One evening, when I went up to Naomi again for
prayer, she challenged me and explained that she
wouldn't pray with me until I had processed every
previous prayer on this issue of unforgiveness and
until I was completely ready to forgive my dad.

I went away and spent time praying and processing and returned to Naomi some time later. When she asked me again if I was ready to completely forgive Dad I said 80 per cent ready. Again, she said unless I was 100 per cent ready and willing to forgive him then we would not pray. Naomi explained to me the importance of forgiveness and how unforgiveness is going to keep me frustrated, burdened and stuck in my faith. She also said that I need to forgive Dad because God has forgiven me of so much in my life, like it says in Colossians 3:13, "Forgive as the Lord forgave you" [NIVUK].

Again, I went away and really thought about why I was holding onto unforgiveness, frustration and anger. I studied Colossians 3:13, Matthew 6:14 and Ephesians 4:32 and began to see and understand that if I don't forgive Dad then I won't move forward in my faith and I will always feel burdened and harbour negativity towards him whenever I see him or talk to him.

Some time passed and again I returned to Naomi for prayer, but this time I was completely ready to forgive Dad and surrender all my previous frustration and anger towards him to God. I prayed first and repented and honestly spoke to God again about my feelings. Then Naomi prayed.

Since that evening, I feel so free, unburdened and happy. My relationship with my dad is much more relaxed and open. And even though I've never told Dad about my frustration and anger towards him, there is so much more joy and freedom in our relationship and love for one another, and I truly believe that is because of the power of forgiveness and God's healing. I even get opportunities now, unlike before, to talk to Dad about my faith. We even talk about his beliefs and the Bible.

Cassie's story highlights the importance of surrendering our wills to God's perfect will. When we encourage people to surrender to God and give him all the rubbish they are holding on to, we will see breakthrough and blessing in their lives that can be achieved no other way.

ENCOURAGING LOVE

Everything we do should be underlined by love. All over the world, people are searching for love. For many, the search proves elusive, but as Christians we know it can be found in God because God's very nature is love. Every action, word, and thought we express should be filled with the divine love of our Saviour, Jesus Christ. We are commanded to love and Christ has shown us how to do this:

> Let no debt remain outstanding, except the continuing debt to love one another, for whoever loves others has fulfilled the law. The commandments, 'You shall not commit adultery,' 'You shall not murder,' 'You shall not steal,' 'You shall not covet,' and whatever other command there may be, are summed up in this one command: 'Love your

> neighbour as yourself.' Love does no harm
> to a neighbour. Therefore love is the fulfil-
> ment of the law.
>
> Romans 13:8–10 (NIVUK)

Love is the fulfilment of the law. If we do everything out of love, we cannot break the commandments; we fulfil them. What a perfect command is the law to love.

For a brush-up on the command to love, go back and read Chapter 5.

ENCOURAGING PRAYER

Praying for the people you disciple is essential. I make an effort to pray daily for the people I am discipling. I occasionally ask them if there is anything they would like specific prayer for. Asking what they need prayer for can be quite enlightening as real needs and worries surface, which may not be disclosed in your regular mentoring sessions. Offering prayer in this way gives them a model to copy as they in turn disciple others. Praying like this should be the practice of every discipler.

John Wesley said, "God will do nothing on earth except in answer to believing prayer." We have a part to play in the world's order and it starts first with us and God, and then the real ripple effect begins as we pray for those around us. Prayer can have a wonderful knock-on effect as we see God impact the people around us by our prayers. Their circle of friends will most likely contain people we don't know and so the blessings of our prayers are manifold. It is exciting to know that the prayers we pray for others can have a much wider impact that we could ever imagine. It's like asking for a pair of socks for Christmas and getting the iPad you've always wanted instead. Don't underestimate the power of praying for others. Only eternity will tell of the many answers to prayer of just one individual.

ENCOURAGING DISCIPLE-MAKING

I get scared to death when I see people who say they've found Jesus Christ, and they're out there, and I wonder, who's teaching them? Who's mentoring them?

Willie Aames[54]

We can talk about evangelism and organise films, discussion groups, drama and anything else, but none of these is any substitute for the daily unspectacular witness of the rank and file Christian.[55]

Before Jesus ascended to heaven, he told his disciples to go make disciples of every nation. That great commissioning is for every one of us too. As others have sown into our lives the gospel of Jesus Christ by investing their time and energy into discipling us, we should likewise seek to do the same for others. We don't have to be highly skilled; in fact, we may only be a little further ahead in our faith. What matters most is that we recognise the need to help someone else just as we have been helped. If every member of a church determines to do this, their church will be spiritually healthy and ready for anything.

Jason is a young man in our church who has learned a lot about making disciples over his six years of attending regen. Here he shares his insightful views on the importance of discipleship:

> My experiences of mentoring in 1:1 and group settings as part of roles in church leadership training have been pivotal to my personal discipleship and have enabled me to grow enormously in my personal relationship with Christ. They have provided a safe place for me to learn from those who are further along in their faith. This has also been the context for challenge and encouragement and a space to allow Jesus to use others to build up and refine me.

> I've had the (sometimes painful) privilege of mentors and those with the responsibility of having pastoral oversight in my life speak the truth even when it has been difficult to hear. I know that particularly in the year after I finished university, being open to learn and listen as a mentee allowed God to do significant work in my heart, engaging with issues around how I saw others and myself. These experiences laid the groundwork for being able to lead in a similar capacity by making disciples.

My journey with those who are more seasoned in their walk with Christ has helped inform my understanding of Scripture and its application. This in turn has allowed me to evaluate my experiences of walking with Jesus and has equipped me with the necessary tools needed for mentoring and discipleship.

You may not believe you have a skill set to be a great discipler like Jason; don't worry. The Holy Spirit is the best educator there is. All he requires is that we are open to his leading and obedient to his call. He will help you every step of the way. If you are in doubt about how to do this, speak to the person who is helping you along in your journey and they can point you in the right direction to helping others.

ENCOURAGING GOOD PRACTICE

A man may be very sincere in good principles, without having good practice.

Samuel Johnson[56]

In his blog, 'Church, Life and Leadership,' Pastor Peter Haas gives an acronym for five aspects of biblical fellowship which frame a healthy picture of what good practice looks like when we seek to come together for spiritual development:

"S.P.A.C.E." is a word that represents five key aspects of Biblical fellowship. Of course, we probably could have picked 12 themes; but, to keep it simple, we focused on the following five ingredients: "Same gender, Prayer, Accountability, and Confession with people of Equal passion.

- S= Same Gender: 2 Samuel 1:26 (like David & Jonathan) Proverbs 27:17 (men sharpening men)

- P= Prayer: James 5:15, 16b; Luke 11: 5–11; 18:1

- A= Accountability i.e., challenging you; setting goals: Proverbs 27:17

- C= Confession: James 5:16; 1 John 1:9; Matthew 6:14–15

- E= Equally Yoked in Passion: Proverbs 13:20; 1 Cor. 15:33; 2 Cor. 6:14ff"[57]

These five ingredients of biblical fellowship are essential to the healthy spiritual growth of every church. Remove one of them and the whole thing may come down like a pack of cards. Good practice keeps people safe and is a good indicator that we take the great commission seriously.

ENCOURAGING CONFIDENTIALITY

A gossip goes around telling secrets, but those who are trustworthy can keep a confidence.

Proverbs 11:13 (NLT)

> Do to others what you want them to do to you. This
> is the meaning of the law of Moses and the teaching
> of the prophets.

Jesus, Matthew 7:12

Love and trust is the glue that holds healthy relationships together. Without trust, there will be suspicion, secrets, and possibly lies too. Confidentiality is a key factor in ensuring a discipling relationship thrives. When people know they can trust someone else with their innermost secrets, it brings a sense of wholeness and being loved that cannot be obtained any other way. Ruth and I don't have any secrets in our marriage. We tell one another everything. It hasn't always been like this, but the more we have come to trust one another, the greater the level our self-disclosures has been. It is without exception that the depth to which we are known will equal the depth to which we can be loved.

When someone trusts you enough to share their innermost thoughts and feelings, that is a sacred thing which should not be taken lightly. I was once jealous of someone who had a particular talent I didn't have. I mistakenly disclosed the green-eyed monster to that person as a means of confession. I wasn't really confident they would respect a confidence, but I unwisely shared my feelings anyway. I later heard their friend had spoken about my jealousy, saying I was like King Saul who became jealous of David – her opinion was that her friend was King

David in the scenario (1 Samuel 18:1–16). I felt the cruel sting of that betrayal and immediately learned two lessons. In future, I wouldn't share confidences with people I didn't trust, and I would carefully hold the sacred confidences people entrusted to me. In a small way, I experienced how a breach of confidence can feel for someone who has experienced a betrayal of sacred trust.

Good practice dictates we respect a person's right to confidentiality. The only exception to breaking a confidence would be for reasons of child or vulnerable adult protection, or if the person disclosing is at risk of harming themselves. If a person begins to disclose anything relating to child abuse or abuse of a vulnerable adult, you will have to inform them that you are not able to maintain confidentiality in that instance. Everyone should know who the Officer for Safeguarding at their church is should they ever need to take advice or report a Safeguarding issue.

EIGHTEEN

ON THE BOX

... left to ourselves we lapse into a kind of collusion with entropy, acquiescing in the general belief that things may be getting worse but that there's nothing much we can do about them. And we are wrong. Our task in the present...is to live as resurrection people in between Easter and the final day, with our Christian life, corporate and individual, in both worship and mission, as a sign of the first and a foretaste of the second.[58]

N. T. Wright

The reward for work well done is the opportunity to do more.

Jonas Salk.[59]

THERE ARE 1,042 REFERENCES TO 'go' in the Bible and only sixty-four references to 'stay'. This fact alone should form our theology nicely, but there is a lot more to say about mission and how it marries well with effective discipleship.

The majority of this book is about our need to get ourselves in gear with good discipleship in following Jesus. It does need to be said that there is more to our spiritual life than just being good followers of Jesus. We need to go and we need to tell. This is the urgent mandate Jesus gave to his disciples before he disappeared into the clouds forty days after his resurrection.

> "Go into all the world and preach the gospel
> to every creature".

Mark 16:15 (NKJV)

That was quite a big ask, I should say is quite a big ask since Jesus' commission to the disciples then still demands our obedience today.

Jesus never rested on his laurels in his mission on earth. You will notice when reading about Jesus' ministry that he seemed to be constantly on the move. He healed people, told them the good news of the gospel and then he was off to the next town or village. Sometimes people begged Jesus to stay, but he told them he had more work to be doing. Other times it was the other way around and people angrily compelled him to leave their towns and villages.

Jesus taught his followers many things; he also prepared them for mission, sent them out into mission and when they returned he discussed with them how things went and encouraged them in what they had done. You can read about how he did it in Luke 10:1–24.

I recently realised that I have been doing the same with Callum. I asked him to share in his own words what that looked like.

> In the summer of 2016 I had the privilege to partake in a mission trip to Romania with Scripture Union. We were based around two hours outside Timisoara. The aim of the mission trip was to host an adventure camp for church kids in Romania. This involved lots of games, hikes, but most importantly, times to worship and pray. As part of my role I had the opportunity to deliver two talks which turned into three. The focus being on the journey of faith and linking it to the adventure camp. Other than some street evangelism, I had never preached before, especially not with a Romanian translator. But I knew it was a calling I needed to step into.
>
> Within one of our mentoring sessions prior to the trip, James gave me wisdom on not only how to structure and write a talk, but he also helped me go through the prayer of salvation so that I would be able to lead others to Jesus should the situation arise. This was definitely necessary as it allowed me to have a starting point with the talk; having a simple structure helped me to have a check list of the components that were needed in a solid, evangelical talk. Not only that, but I had a phone conversation with James the day before my flight where he gave me pointers about Romanian translation and how to stop

and pause your thoughts while the previous sentence is being translated. Again this was really helpful as it gave me more confidence when actually speaking over the course of that week.

During the trip, contact was limited due to poor phone signal; however, we still kept up with our Bible reading when signal was gained, which allowed us to communicate, and for me to tell James how things went. This meant that James' prayers for each could be more specific; not just me, but for the whole team.

After returning from the mission trip, James and I had another opportunity in mentoring where we could celebrate the amazing things that God had been doing in the week, not just in my faith, but in the faith of the young people I had ministered to as well. Our time of reflection on what happened in Romania gave me great opportunity to get critical when looking back on my talks. What did I do well? What could be slightly changed for the next time I have the privilege of speaking? Ultimately, having James help me through the mission trip with advice, prayer and wisdom was a huge confidence boost to me.

What Callum experienced on that mission trip was definitely helpful for him in his engagement with Christian discipleship. His opportunity to prepare, and later reflect on all that happened in Romania, deepened his understanding of mission and gave him a greater appreciation for good preparation and reflection regarding mission. Thorough preparation, good practice and healthy reflection will help make our mission far more effective in the both the short and the long-term.

One of our church's opportunities for mission is good old-fashioned street outreach. We set up a simple box in the middle of Romford and we give anyone who wants to, the opportunity to preach to passers-by. Sometimes we get really good engagement with people and other times, not so much. Regardless, we keep on doing it.

One of our interns was very reticent to get on the box and I encouraged her to give it a go. I said, "Even if you get up and say, 'Jesus loves you', that will be a start." She wasn't having any of it. She said she wasn't ready to do it, she wasn't prepared, her throat was hurting, she didn't have anything to say. I gave up trying to persuade her and turned to engage with some other people standing nearby, only to hear her speaking from the box with great conviction and power a few minutes later. To say I was surprised would be an understatement. I learned that day that we need to encourage people to step up in mission even if we get little or no positive feedback. Sometimes people need just a little nudge. It is amazing what happens when we encourage people to step out for God in mission.

Jesus commands us to 'go'. Let's be sure we are putting our best foot forward as we follow his lead.

NINETEEN

THE PERFECT MENTOR

There is no microwave for discipleship, there is just the long slow road of transformation.

Will van der Hart[60]

WHEN I WAS NEW TO DISCIPLING PEOPLE, I believed with the right amount of love and care I could make anyone stick close to God and go on to become a sterling example of what a great Christian should look like. My modus operandi spectacularly set me up for some bitter disappointments. I figured if I worked hard enough at discipling them, they would never backslide or become lukewarm. How mistaken and misguided I was. More than once I was reduced to tears after discovering a mentee had fallen away from God and chosen to go their own way. It was utterly devastating and heartbreaking for me.

After struggling with feeling like a complete failure, the ancient story of Adam and Eve came to mind. That perfect couple, in the perfect garden, had the best 'mentor' anyone could hope for: God himself. What happened? They chose to disobey God's instructions and do what was right in their own eyes. The serpent deceived Eve to eat from the Tree of Knowledge of Good and Evil, and Adam wilfully sinned by partaking too. The resulting consequence of their wilful disobedience bought them a one-way ticket out of the Garden of Eden forever. Not good.

God, the perfect Father, the greatest 'mentor', was not able to ensure those he loved would not choose to go their own way. Because of my skewed understanding of what I could and could not achieve in a mentoring rela-tionship, I had lost sight of the truth that everyone has a choice. I could not live people's lives for them. Sometimes I've wished I could have when I've seen them self-destruct because of the bad choices they have made. Nevertheless, this is the way it has to be if we are to experience free will. We may not like the wrong choices others make, but we can be ready to pick up the pieces when the people we love choose to go the wrong way and eventually discover that sin is not the way to real joy and true freedom. There will be no need for "I told you so"s. Remembering our own struggles and failures helps us to humbly lead them back to the cross – that old rugged cross of grace. It is from there we lovingly encourage them to begin again, with healing for their souls and resurrection hope in their hearts. The journey of discipleship is life-long; the journey will be hard at times, but take heart, the journey is shared.

TWENTY

ALL DOES NOT YET GLEAM
−49 YEARS, 7 MONTHS AND
26 DAYS

God is strong and can help you not to fall. He can bring you before his glory without any wrong in you and can give you great joy.

Jude 24

The "show business," which is so incorporated into our view of Christian work today, has caused us to drift far from Our Lord's conception of discipleship. It is instilled in us to think that we have to do exceptional things for God; we have not. We have to be exceptional in ordinary things, to be holy in mean streets, among mean people, surrounded by sordid sinners. That is not learned in five minutes.

Oswald Chambers[61]

Martin Luther was a monk who had a life-transforming revelation of the grace of God. He wrote the following about the process of sanctification, which should give hope to anyone who has the feeling they have not yet 'arrived':

This life therefore is not righteousness but growth in righteousness;

Not health but healing;

Not being but becoming;

Not rest but exercise.

We are not yet what we shall be, but we are growing toward it.

The process is not finished, but it is going on.

This is not the end, but it is the road.

All does not yet gleam in glory, but all is being purified.[62]

Yes, Martin, what encouraging words. We don't become like Jesus in one day. Becoming is a process. I often want the refining process finished straight away. Becoming is a sometimes painful business, but the result is worth it. There is nothing that can compare with being like Jesus.

One of my favourite Bible verses is Galatians 2:20. The apostle Paul says:

> I was put to death on the cross with Christ,
> and I do not live anymore – it is Christ who
> lives in me. I still live in my body, but I live
> by faith in the Son of God who loved me
> and gave himself to save me.

I want to understand more what this means on my journey of discipleship. If I really comprehend that I have been 'put to death' with Christ on the cross, I will rest in the simple truth that the only way to live for him is by faith – faith in Jesus Christ, not faith in the life of James Poch. At the time of writing this, it has been 49 years, 7 months and 26 days since I gave my heart to Jesus. Life has not always been easy-going for me, but I can confidently say it has been an adventure and one I wouldn't trade for anything.

There will always be tremendous highs, brutal struggles and everything else in between on the road to becoming like Jesus. I want to encourage you, whether you are at the start, middle or end of your journey with Jesus Christ, to keep going. Keep on keeping on with him, do all he asks you to do and take as many people along with you as you can. We are all on the road that Martin Luther talked about – the journey of discipleship.

Jesus didn't promise us that we wouldn't face setbacks and hardship, they will certainly come, but he promised us his presence. He promised he would never leave us or forsake us. What more could we ask for on the road to glory?

APPENDIX

MENTORING – THE FIRST MEETING

When starting a mentoring or accountability relationship, it is a good idea to have a few guidelines and boundaries in place which will help things run smoothly for both people. From the outset, we suggest the person seeking to be in a mentoring partnership approaches the person responsible for discipleship at church. It is helpful for us to know who is looking after who so we can safeguard the smooth running of partnerships. To keep things simple, we recommend same gender partnerships. This provides some protection against opportunities for temptation.

Ensure the partnership is open-ended, allowing for either person to opt out if things don't gel. We recommend giving it at least three months and suggest people meet up every three or four weeks. If after three months things are going well, you may wish to review how things are going every six months.

Discuss exactly how mutual confidentiality will work between you.

Always pray at the beginning and end of meetings, asking the Holy Spirit to seal the work he has been doing, and pray for continued blessing on the partnership.

Try to be comprehensive when discussing problems, issues and challenges. Discipleship is not about policing sin, it is about calling out destiny. There may be occasions where it will be helpful to talk about things such as lust issues, financial problems and relationship concerns, but what will be far more beneficial will be discussing how growth in understanding the grace of God is developing and how the practice of the spiritual disciplines are coming on. When these are in place the lust issues and other problems will be far more manageable.

Don't undermine the role of another mentor. When we see people struggling who are being mentored by someone else, it might be tempting to give them a bit of advice or direction. This may be problematic, given that we don't fully know the background story. A piece of advice given to someone's mentee, however well-intentioned, may undo a considerable amount of work on the part of that person's mentor. The best possible action is to be praying for the person and ask the Lord to give wisdom to their mentor and refer them back to their mentor or discipler.

At the beginning of any discipling relationship, both parties should form an agreement on boundaries, how often to meet and the length of the discipleship relationship. Never start without first letting someone know they can end the partnership at any time; however, the expectation would be to meet for at least six months and potentially up to one year, at which time you can review how everything is going. No one should ever feel trapped in a discipling relationship. A light touch is essential for a healthy discipling rapport.

Frequency of meetings with people we disciple may vary. Monthly meetings work well for some, while I find that meeting fortnightly with some of the men I disciple is about right for most of them. Anything more than this can be a little excessive. People need space to grow and live out what they are learning in their personal Bible devotions, church life and discipleship meetings.

IF A MENTORING/ACCOUNTABILITY PARTNERSHIP ISN'T WORKING

A partnership which isn't working well can be extremely frustrating. The first thing to do is to bring the problem out into the open. Discuss what is working well and what isn't. Would a change of time or venue make meeting up better, or is the problem more to do with personality differences? It may be the expectations of the discipler are too high, or in some instances, considered too low; there may not be enough challenge to keep meetings fresh and stimulating. Tweaking and changing how you work together can give new life to a mentoring relationship that is feeling a bit stale. If nothing improves, it is probably best for both concerned that the partnership ends. A great dynamic in a mentoring relationship is an essential ingredient for a dynamic synergy.

Occasionally there will be times when every problem has been analysed and dissected to death, every prayer has been prayed and every solution we can think of has been applied, but with little benefit or change. When faced with situations like this, we need to refer people on to others who are more experienced and qualified. We are not called to be anyone's saviour. Our role in helping others is not about us. We are simply servants to one another.

You may contact the author at holygrit@regen.church

END NOTES

1   Dietrich Bonhoeffer, *The Cost of Discipleship* (New York: Touchstone, 1995), 59.

2   Brad Bridges, @bradbridges, *Twitter* (13/07/2014).

3   Dallas Willard, *The Great Omission: Reclaiming Jesus's Essential Teachings on Discipleship* (Oxford: Monarch Books 2006), 1.

4   C.S. Lewis, *Mere Christianity* (New York: Macmillan, 1943), 154.

5   Pete Greig, @PeteGreig, *Twitter* (26/06/2014).

6   John Piper, http://www.desiringgod.org/messages/he-set-his-face-to-go-to-jerusalem, Accessed 30/6/17.

7   Elisabeth Elliot, *Passion and Purity: Learning to Bring Your Love Life Under Christ's Control* (Grand Rapids: Fleming H. Revell, 2002), 73.

8   Karl Rahner, https://www.brainyquote.com/quotes/quotes/k/karlrahner204839.html,Accessed 30/6/17.

9   Brennan Manning, *The Ragamuffin Gospel* (Colorado Springs: Multnomah 2005), 115.

10   Rotten Reviews cited in Noah Lukeman, *The First Five Pages* (Oxford: Oxford University Press, 2010), 180.

11   A.W. Tozer, *Culture*, (Chicago: Moody, 2016), 26.

12   Bishop Graham Cray, http://www.freshexpressions.org. uk/news/grahamcray-discipleship, Accessed 30/6/17.

13   Michael Spencer, *Mere Churchianity: Finding Your Way Back to Jesus-Shaped Spirituality* (Colorado Springs: Crown Publishing Group, 2010), 101.

14   Nicky Gumbel, *Twitter* (08/04/2014).

15   Ann Landers, http://www.dictionary-quotes.com/love-is-friendship-that-has-caught-fire-it-is-quiet-understanding-mutual-confidence-sharing-and-forgiving-it-is-loyalty-through-good-and-bad-times-it-settles-for-less-than-perfec-tion-and-ma/, Accessed 30/6/17.

16   Jack Canfield, Mark Victor Hansen, *A Third Serving of Christian Soup for the Soul* (New York: Random House, 2010, ebrary), 246.

17   John Wesley, sermon on "Causes of the Inefficacy of Christianity," in his *Sermons on Several Occasions,* 2 vols (New York: Waugh and Mason, 1836), 1:437.

18   Mary Pytches, *A Child No More* (Chorleywood: Kingdom Power Trust Publications, 2005), 15.

19   Dallas Willard, *The Spirit of the Disciplines: Understanding How God Changes Lives*, (New York: HarperCollins Publishers, 1988)

20   Richard Foster, The *Celebration of Discipline,* (London: Hodder and Stoughton, 2008)

21   Ibid 175

22   Adapted from Bill Donahue, *Leading Life-Changing Small Groups* (Grand Rapids: Zondervan Publishing House, 1996), 51-52.

23   http://www.christianitytoday.com/ct/2002/december-web-only/12-16-55.0.html, Accessed 30/6/17.

24   Brennan Manning, *The Furious Longing of God* (Colorado Springs: David C Cook, 2009), 86.

25   Twitter (06/04/2014).

26   Lee Camp, *Mere Discipleship: Radical Christianity in a Rebellious World*, (Grand Rapids: Brazos Press, 2008), 27.

27   Dietrich Bonheoffer, *Life Together* (New York: Harper and Row, 1954), 112.

28   Corrie Ten Boom, Elizabeth Sherrill, John Sherrill, *The Hiding Place* (Boston: Hachette, 2012), 31.

29   T.D. Jakes, *OPRAH'S LIFECLASS*, http://www.oprah.com/oprahs-lifeclass/Bishop-TD-Jakes-Says-Dont-Dwell-on-Your-History-Video_1, Accessed 30/6/17.

30   Winston Churchill, *Speech*, (The Royal College of Physicians),London, March 2nd 1944.

31   Anthony de Mello, *One Minute Wisdom*, (New York: Bantam Doubleday Dell, 1985).

32   Brennan Manning, *The Ragamuffin Gospel: Good News for the Bedraggled, Beat-Up, and Burnt Out* (Colorado Springs: Crown Publishing Group, 2008), 12.

33   http://www.thesun.co.uk/sol/homepage/showbiz/bizarre/4285973/Atheist-actress-Keira-Knightley-wishes-she-believed-in-God.html, Accessed 30/6/17.

34   Aleksandr Solzhenitsyn, *The Gulag Archipelago 1918–1956* (New York: Fontana, 1974).

35   *The Times Saturday Magazine* (06/01/2001).

36   Mark Twain, *Mark Twain's Notebook*, (1935 Ed) 347.

37   John F. Kennedy, *State of the Union Address,* 1961.

38   http://billygraham.org/devotion/the-importance-of-cor-porate-worship/comment-page-1/, Accessed 30/6/17.

39   Rick Warren, *The Purpose Driven Life*, (Grand Rapids: Zondervan, 2002), 172. Rick is quoting Ephesians 4:22 from The Message

40   Hugh Rawson; Margaret Miner, *The Oxford Dictionary of American Quotations* (Oxford: Oxford University Press, 2008), 3.

41   http://www.nbcnews.com/video/meet-the-press/44660270 #44660270

42   Timothy Keller, *The Meaning of Marriage: Facing the Complexities of Commitment with the Wisdom of God* (London: Hodder and Stoughton, 2013), 89.

43   Peter Scazerro, *Emotionally Healthy Spirituality*, (Nashville:Thomas Nelson, 2011)

44   Michael Harrison, *A Book of Very Short Poems,* (Oxford: Oxford University Press, 2001), 60.

45   Johann Wolfgang von Goethe, *Goethe's Opinions on the World, Mankind, Literature, Science and Art* (London: John W. Parker and Son, 1853) 55.

46   Brennan Manning, *The Furious Longing of God,* (Colorado Springs: David C Cook, 2009), 83.

47   http://www.theage.com.au/articles/2004/02/08/107585 4124922.html

48   http://www.brainyquote.com/quotes/quotes/c/charlessta451688.html?src=t_destiny, Accessed 30/6/17.

49   Harriet B. Braiker, *Who's Pulling Your Strings? How to Break the Cycle of Manipulation and Regain Control of Your Life* (Columbus, OH: McGraw-Hill Education, 2004), 42.

50   M. Scott Peck, *The Different Drum – Community Making and Peace* (London: Arrow Books, 1990), 88.

51   *Momentum Mini Mag* (Soul Survivor, Early Spring 2012), 15.

52   Christian Smith and Melinda Lundquist Denton, *Soul Searching: The Religious and Spiritual Lives of American Teenagers* (adapted from Wiki, 2005).

53   Elizabeth Elliot, *A Lamp Unto my Feet: The Bible's Light for Your Daily Walk* (Ventura, CA: Gospel Light Publications, 2004), 186.

54   https://www.brainyquote.com/quotes/quotes/w/willieaame289593.html, Accessed 30/6/17.

55   David Watson, Grow and Flourish, *A Daily Guide to Growth and Renewal* (Wheaton, IL: Harold Shaw Publishers, 1982), 95.

56   James Boswell, John Wilson Croker, *The Life of Samuel Johnson, LLD.D.* (London: John Murray, 1821), 55.

57   Peter Haas, *How to Find Transformational Fellowship* (http://www.peterhaas.org/?p=1415, 22/09/2014), Accessed 30/6/17.

58   N. T. Wright, *Surprised by Hope: Rethinking Heaven, the Resurrection, and the Mission of the Church* (New York: Harper, 2008), 29-30.

59   Dennis Denenberg and Lorraine Roscoe, *50 American Heroes Every Kid Should Meet!* (Brookfield, CT: Millbrook Press, 2001), 99.

60   Will van der Hart, *Twitter* (29/05/2014).

61   Oswald Chambers, *Daily Thoughts for Disciples*, (Fort Washington, PA: Christian Literature Crusade, 1976), 141.

62   Martin Luther, *Defence of All the Articles*, Lazareth transl., as found in Grace Brame, *Receptive Prayer* (Atlanta: Chalice Press, 1985), 119.

Lightning Source UK Ltd.
Milton Keynes UK
UKHW02f2150130318
319351UK00002B/64/P